Collecting
Art Plastic
Jewelry

Leigh Leshner

Identification and Price Guide

©2005 Leigh Leshner
Published by

kp books
An imprint of F+W Publications, Inc.

**700 East State Street • Iola, WI 54990-0001
715-445-2214 • 888-457-2873**

Our toll-free number to place an order or obtain
a free catalog is (800) 258-0929.

Library of Congress Catalog Number: 2004113677

ISBN: 0-87349-954-9

Designed by Kay Sanders
Edited by Tracy L. Schmidt

Printed in the United States of America

Acknowledgments

I wish to thank my parents, Robert and Carol Leshner, for always being there for me and encouraging me and inspiring me to do my best.

Thanks also to: Vintage Fashion and Costume Jewelry editor Lucille Tempesta, author Marcia Brown, and dealer/collector Barbara Wood for their editorial expertise.

Maurice Childs for his extraordinary photography.

Marcia Brown, Judy Clarke, Ann Eliason, Jim Foltz, Barbara Harris, Karen Kennedy, Lori Kizer, Karen Kronimus, Carol Leshner, Janet Lawwill, Kristin Martinez, Elizabeth Rowlands, BeeGee McBride, Sheri Peti, Jackie Weeks, and Barbara Wood for providing jewelry from their private collections.

My editor Tracy Schmidt, page designer Kay Sanders, and acquisitions editor Paul Kennedy.

Special thanks go to Maurice Childs for his extraordinary photography.

Contents

*Left: contemporary hard plastic cuff with rhinestones, **$30**;
right: contemporary hard plastic bangles with rhinestones, **$24** each.*

Introduction

Art plastic jewelry has been a favorite of collectors for decades. This book will feature jewelry made from the various types of plastics: celluloid, Bakelite, Lucite, thermoplastics, and thermoset plastics.

Plastic jewelry is often referred to as novelty jewelry, because it was fun and whimsical. Designers have used the relatively inexpensive material to create all types of jewelry from necklaces and rings to pins and bangles. Each piece is unique, reflecting the designer's desire to bring life to the jewelry through the use of color and carvings.

The number of collectors has grown tremendously. Most people know what Bakelite is and the pieces on the market are both collectible and valuable. In fact, many special pieces bring prices in the thousands of dollars. With this increased interest, people want to know how to tell the difference between the different types of plastics, the history behind the jewelry, and what it is worth. This book will provide you with the answers to these questions.

Lady brooch, resin, $275.

Evans wave bangles, resin, $200 each.

History

Plastikos is a Greek word meaning to mold or to form, and that is the perfect description for the material we commonly refer to as plastic. Plastic is a material that generally can be shaped and molded under heat and pressure. Plastics come in all colors from clear to vibrant hues of fuchsia, red, and orange to more subdued colors of black, brown, and avocado.

There are two types of plastics: thermoplastic and thermoset. A thermoset can be reheated and reshaped such as acrylic, gutta-percha, and polyethylene. A thermoplastic is a plastic that is heated, causing a chemical reaction. The plastic is then shaped into an object that permanently hardens and becomes heat resistant. Melamine and Bakelite are thermoplastics.

Plastics have been used for purposes of all kinds ranging from radio casings to furniture to other utilitarian purposes. It has also been used to make jewelry. Everything you could imagine: necklaces, bracelets, pins, dress clips, rings, earrings, buckles, buttons, and bangles. Often pieces would be made entirely out of plastic, while at other times, plastic was used simply to accent a piece. Because of World War II, the use of pot metal (the tin and lead used in pot metal) was prohibited for use other than for the military.

Designers began using other materials to make fun and fanciful jewelry that put a smile on the wearer's face. Necklaces varied from plain to carved. There were simple bead necklaces, pendants, charm necklaces, faceted necklaces, necklaces made of fruits and vegetables, and necklaces with rhinestones. There were bangles accented with various materials such as rhinestones, metal and hand painting. They were carved, reverse carved and injected with flowers, bugs, and other items. There were hinged cuffs, two-tone bangles, polka dots, gumdrops, striped, marbled, bow tie, stretch bracelets, and charm bracelets. Brooches ranged from plain to detailed and ornate to articulated, so that parts of the pin actually moved.

*Thermoset plastic bangles, **$75** each.*

*Carved Bakelite bangles, from left: marbeled green, red, and black, **$395** each.*

*Reverse-carved Lucite butterfly brooch and earrings, **$85**.*

Prison rings received their distinctive name because inmates in prison would take a toothbrush, a shaving brush or a pen and melt it down. They would then use celluloid to bond it together. They would often add pictures onto the ring's front.

Plastics are not limited to jewelry. The material has been used for umbrellas, ring boxes, jewelry boxes, purses, decorative items, radios, household items, furniture, and just about everything you can imagine! Manufacturers loved the easily handled material, and the ability to mechanize the production process. Store owners loved the low wholesale price of the items. Shoppers, in turn, smiled at the finished item and happily paid the small bill.

In the 1920s, celluloid, a popular material, was used to create jewelry that used geometric designs, Egyptian motifs, oriental motifs, as well as art-deco designs that were streamlined and modern. Often the art-deco designs were mixed with chrome and rhinestones. Europeans used galalith in their jewelry combining it with chrome, brass, silver, and gold plating to create avant-garde and art-deco designs.

In the 1930s, Bakelite was used to create whimsical and fun jewelry that incorporated designs of fruits, vegetables, animals, figurals, flowers, cameos, and geometric designs.

In the 1940s, materials were scarce because of wartime production. However, Bakelite and other plastics were plentiful. Because the material was inexpensive, designers indulged in their fantasies and created pieces that gave life to an outfit for a relatively small price tag. In fact, the pieces were not only found in the high-end department stores like Bergdorf-Goodman and Lord and Taylor, but they were also abundant in dime stores.

Plastic jewelry has continued to be made throughout the years. Many designers have incorporated plastic elements into their jewelry such as Kenneth Lane, Coro, Trifari, Hobé, Eisenberg, Lisner, and a host of others.

Currently, there are designers who are making wonderful items by designing and carving pieces of jewelry from old materials. This process is a lost art that is now being resurrected by a few select artisans whose work incorporates old methods with a breath of fresh air and design innovation.

Prices of plastic jewelry vary. The handmade modern pieces of jewelry can be expensive because of the amount of the intricate work and time needed for production. The prices of older pieces vary depending upon scarcity, rarity, condition, quality, and popularity. The more detailed and intricately carved, the more expensive it will be. But don't let this discourage you from collecting. There are still affordable pieces to be found. If you are looking for some fun, inexpensive pieces to wear, there are a lot of imported plastic and Lucite pieces.

*Raised dot Bakelite bangles with rhinestones, from left: marbled green and orange, marbled tobacco brown and butterscotch, dark marbled blue green with light green, **$600** each.*

*Double ring holder, Bakelite, **$550.***

*Top: Bakelite prison ring with photo, **$150**;*
*Bottom: Bakelite prison ring, **$225**.*

*Lisner brooch, earring and bracelet set, molded plastic, **$95**.*

Types of Plastic

There are two kinds of plastics: natural and synthetic. Natural plastics are those that have evolved through either the natural biological process or are natural materials such as amber, horn, tortoiseshell, gutta-percha, and vulcanite. Synthetic plastics are those that are manmade with chemicals such as cellulose, Bakelite, casein, and Lucite. A variation of this is semi-synthetics, which occur when you modify the chemical composition of natural materials such as casein, celluloid, cellulose acetate, ebonite, Parkisene, and vulcanized rubber. When we talk about plastics today, we are generally speaking of manmade synthetic plastics.

Natural Plastics

Amber: Amber is a fossilized resin from trees indigenous to the Baltic Coast known as Pinites Succinifer. This material ranges in color from pale yellow to black. It is translucent, and sometimes dust particles are visible in the material.

Horn: Horn is a natural substance that comes from the tusks and horns of animals. The substance is ground, pressed, and heated. When it is heated, horn becomes transparent and a pale yellow color. From 1770 to 1880, one of the primary uses of horn was for hair combs.

Tortoiseshell: Tortoiseshell comes from the hawksbill turtle. The shell is an organic substance that is ground, pressed, and then heated.

Gutta-percha: In 1843, while in Malaysia, Dr. Mongomerie discovered that the natural material scraped by hand from the Palaquium trees was used to make many items. The substance, in its natural form, was hard and inelastic. But when it was placed in hot water it softened, and could then be pressed into shapes for a variety of uses. In the 19th century, gutta-percha was used for household items, frames, jewelry, and gutta-percha golf balls.

Vulcanite: Vulcanite is a molded rubber that is heated with sulphur. When this process is taken to extreme measures, the material becomes vulcanite. In 1843, Thomas Handcock patented the process for vulcanized rubber in England. In 1844, Charles Goodyear patented the process in the United States. These methods involved a process of making the rubber elastic and then as the process continued, the rubber became hard and was able to be molded.

Ebonite: Ebonite was the first semi-synthetic material. It is a molded rubber that is created in a process similar to that of vulcanite.

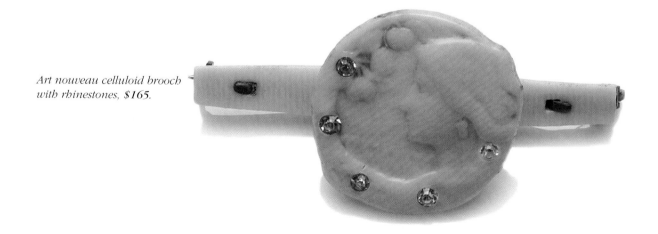

Art nouveau celluloid brooch with rhinestones, $165.

Synthetic Plastics

Celluloid: Celluloid was originally invented in 1855 by Alexander Parkes under the name Parkesine. It was later refined and patented by John Wesley Hyatt in 1869. Two years later, Hyatt formed the American Celluloid Company, which later became a division of the Celanese Corporation. It is also known as Plastacele, so named by E.I. Dupont de Nemours Company of Wilmington, Delaware.

Celluloid is an artificial, semi-synthetic thermoplastic made from pyroxylin and camphor that resembles ivory. It is a thin, lightweight material that is sensitive to heat. It can be softened and re-used. The problem with this early form of celluloid was its high flammability. In 1927, the compound was refined with vinegar being substituted for nitric acid and camphor so that the material would not be flammable. Celluloid comes in over two hundred colors. The material is buffed, polished, carved, and molded to create wonderful pins, necklaces, rings, earrings, bracelets, buckles, and hair accessories.

Galalith: In 1897, Adolph Spitteler was attempting to develop a substitute for horn and he created Galalith. The material was harder than celluloid and could be molded when heated. It was used throughout Europe for buckles, dress clips, jewelry, buttons, pins, and knitting needles. However, the material did have its problems. It tended to warp, and was not strong or moisture resistant.

Galalith is the trade name for casein or milk plastic. It is made from a protein substance derived from sour milk combined with formaldehyde that softens in hot water. The term Galalith is Greek with "Gala" meaning milk and "Litho" meaning stone. It is also known as erinoid, karolith, and aladdinite.

Bakelite: Bakelite was the first man-made plastic. In 1908, Leo H. Baekeland, a chemist, invented a thermoplastic that is commonly known as Bakelite. Bakelite is a synthetic resin that is often combined with fillers like wood flour and asbestos to make it stronger. The material is also known as phenolic, phenolic resin, or phenol formaldehyde. However, the common term most associated with it is Bakelite. In 1910, Baekeland established the General Bakelite Company with branches in Berlin, and later in Great Britain and Canada. In 1938, the company became the plastics division of Union Carbide Company. Originally used as an insulator for electronics, it was soon being used for other purposes. Jewelry made from Bakelite started in the 1930s.

Baekeland had a patent until 1926. In 1930, the American Catalin Corporation developed another phenolic, which they called Catalin. Among his competitors were the Bakelite Corporation and

American Catalin Corporation. In 1935, the Catalin Corporation introduced a clear material known as Prystal. This material turned an amber color and is now referred to as applejuice Bakelite.

Another company that used the material was the Marbelette Company in the 1940s and 1950s. While there are different types of phenolic resins such as Catalin, Prystal, Marbelette, or Durez, it is most common to hear most people refer to the material as Bakelite.

Bakelite will oxidize over the years causing the outer color to change. This generally happens because of exposure to sun and chemicals like perfume, hair spray, and make-up. Often, when the material is sanded down there is a different color inside. Crème-colored Bakelite was originally white; brown was originally lavender; green was turquoise; and orange was pink.

Bakelite was made into rods, tubes, sheets, and slabs that could then be cut, sliced, drilled, sawed, carved, and polished to create various objects.

The carving varied from minor to heavy and with intricate designs. Often it was hand carved, but sometimes a lathe was used. This involved the use of different bits to cut the patterns into the material. The objects were then tumbled and polished. The polishing could also be done by hand with a soft cloth or on a felt wheel using a pumice stone. Sometimes a combination of methods would be used when a piece was carved on a lathe and then finished by hand. A type of finish called "ashing," refers to when a piece was polished with a wet pumice on a lathe equipped with a muslin wheel and then waxed with a compound on a dry muslin wheel.

Bakelite comes in a wide variety of colors:

1. **One color:** There are approximately 100 single colors of Bakelite.
2. **Marbled:** A swirled combination of two or more colors.
3. **Opaque:** A color that is without luster and cannot be seen through.
4. **Translucent:** A color that allows light to pass through it, but is diffused so it is hard to see clearly through the material.
5. **Transparent:** A color that allows light to pass through it and can be seen through.
6. **End of the day:** A combination of colors that were left at the end of the day and then mixed together so no materials were wasted.
7. **Stardust:** Slivers of gold or silver were added to the Bakelite.
8. **Applejuice Bakelite:** A clear Bakelite that turns an amber color.

Examples of Raw Bakelite

Bakelite rods

Bakelite slabs and rods

Bakelite sheets

Bakelite cylinders

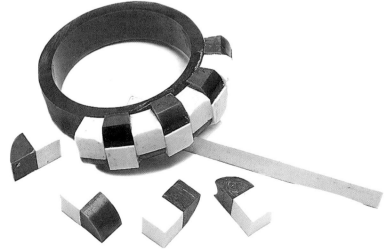

An unfinished Bakelite bangle made
by Karen and Howard Kronimus.

Bakelite was a cheap and colorful material that was used to make jewelry of all kinds: bangles, brooches, necklaces, rings, and earrings. The material was cast, carved, or laminated into floral and geometric designs and whimsical figurals shaped like animals, fruits, hats, fish, and people. Often the jewelry was accented with rhinestones, metal, wood, and Lucite. The material was also hand painted or reverse carved, a method where the Bakelite is carved from the inside so that the design shows on the outside.

Bangles were especially popular, and designers used various methods to create unusual and colorful bracelets.

1. **Carved bangles:** Bakelite bangles were carved with everything from dramatic intricate designs of flowers, leaves, and animals to minor carvings.
2. **Faceted bangles:** The Bakelite was cut to create facets in the material.
3. **Bangles with mixed materials:** The Bakelite was mixed with other materials such as wood, rhinestones, and metals.
4. **Hinged bangles:** A Bakelite tube was cut in half and then attached with a spring-loaded hinge that was secured into the material with screws or pins.
5. **Two-tone-carved bangles:** These bangles had one color inside another color and the top layer was carved so the second color could then be seen.
6. **Reverse-carved bangles:** These bangles were carved on the inside of the transparent bangle and often the bangle would be painted or infused with flowers, fish, dots, animals or geometric designs.
7. **Polka-dot bangles:** These bangles were made by placing a rod of one color inside the tubes of another color and then slicing it. The designer would then grind the piece, tumble it, sand it, and then polish it.
8. **Bow-tie bangles:** The process to make these types of bangles is similar to the polka-dot bangles except that the rod that was inserted into the tube was done at unusual angles that created a bow-tie effect.
9. **Gumdrop bangles:** The process to make these types of bangles is also similar to the polka-dot bangles, except that the rods that were inserted were oddly shaped. These types of bangles were designed and manufactured by Charles Elkaim in the late 1950s.
10. **Striped bangles:** These bangles were made by taking different colors of Bakelite and then bonding them together through lamination with a liquid phenolic resin that acted like a glue.

Acrylic: First developed in 1927, acrylic is a lightweight, petrochemical thermoplastic that was made from acrylic acid or a derivative of it. It is also known as Plexiglas made by the Rohm and Hass Company, and Lucite made by Dupont.

Lucite: In 1937, Dupont introduced a material known as Lucite. Lucite is a clear material but is often tinted with color. Designers used Lucite for jewelry and created wonderful pieces by faceting,

Carved hinged bangle, Bakelite, **$550.**

engraving, molding, and carving the material. They also combined it with wood, leather, ceramic, rhinestones, and metals. Lucite can be clear, tinted, or opaque, with the opaque Lucite often being referred to as moonglow. Carved Lucite and Lucite imbedded with other materials such as glitter, seashells, and rhinestones were popular in the 1950s.

Dupont produced Lucite during World War II for use as windshields in fighter planes. As part of their war efforts, Trifari, a jewelry manufacturer, installed Plexiglas windshields and turrets in military bombers. However, the company would only use flawless materials, leaving excess rejected material. Rather than throw away the leftovers, Alfred Phillipe, the head designer, thought of an ingenious way of using the material by cutting cabochons from the Plexiglas and incorporating them into jewelry designs. These designs are known as "jelly bellies" with the Lucite cabochons as the predominate

feature of the whimsical line of jewelry which includes fish, spiders, elephants, bees, and other creatures. While Trifari called it their "clear line," collectors lovingly refer to them as "jelly bellies."

Plastic Production Methods

There are several production methods used for plastics:
1. **Blow Molding:** This method is used to produce hollow objects by injecting hot air into a plastic tube until the plastic expands to the desired level and forms into the shape of the mold.
2. **Calendering:** This method uses rollers to spread the liquid plastic over another material.
3. **Casting:** This method creates objects by pouring the plastic into a mold and letting it harden.
4. **Impression Molding:** This method uses heat and pressure on the plastic that is placed into a heated clamshell mold. The material is then

Top left: pair of jelly belly turtle fur clips, sterling with rhinestones, $425; bottom left: Coro sterling vermeil jelly belly swan with rhinestones, $295; top right: Trifari sterling vermeil spider jelly belly fur clip with rhinestones, $545; bottom right: Corocraft sterling jelly belly fish with enameling and rhinestones, $495.

freed and it flows around the shape of the mold, sometimes leaving seams in the object.

5. **Extrusion:** This method allows for the production of tubes and filaments by pushing the liquid plastic through a shaped tube.
6. **Injection Molding:** This is a high-speed method of injection molding where the heated plastic is forced into a cold mold.
7. **Laminating:** This method takes the object and passes it through a pair of rollers that apply a coating of melted plastic which then forms a sealed off encapsulation of the object.

There were other variations of bracelets using Bakelite. There were stretchy or elastic bracelets that used drilled pieces of Bakelite that were then strung together with elastic. Charm bracelets were also popular with charms in the shapes of fruit, vegetables, geometric designs, and figurals hanging from chains made of various materials such as celluloid, metal, cord, and other plastics.

Reverse-carved Bakelite bangle, ***$1,200.***

Identification Tests

There are several tests that you can do to help you determine the type of plastic that is being used. This can be done through appearance, smell, heat, and sound tests.

Marks in the material such as seams and mold marks can indicate if the jewelry is made of a thermoset or a thermoplastic. Thermoset plastics will show mold marks and seams whereas Bakelite generally will not.

The original color of the materials often changes over time. Bakelite will oxidize, and often the color on the inside of a bangle will be darker than the outside. Acrylic and celluloid tend to yellow with age. Vulcanite and ebonite have a faint, yellowish cast.

A common test for materials is the smell test. You can get a piece of jewelry hot and then smell it to determine what type of material it is made from. This can be done by rubbing the piece vigorously so that it becomes hot. Be careful when you do this, so that you do not damage the piece. Celluloid smells like camphor and/or mothballs when it is heated. Galalith smells like burnt milk. Bakelite smells like formaldehyde/carbolic acid. Tortoiseshell smell likes burned hair. Vulcanite and ebonite smell like sulphur. Cellulose acetate smells like vinegar.

You can also run a piece of Bakelite under hot water or dip it in boiling water so that the piece gets hot. Then you can smell it. If it smells like carbolic acid then it is Bakelite. Be sure to be careful not to get any accents such as rhinestones on the piece wet when you do this test.

You can place vulcanite and ebonite in a sealed plastic bag for a short while and then smell the bag. There should be a sulphur smell.

Another way to test the material is with a hot needle. I don't recommend this method because it will damage the piece. However, if you want to test the material, you can heat up the tip of a needle and then see if it will go into the material. A hot needle will penetrate a thermoset plastic, but will not penetrate a thermoplastic.

Bakelite can be distinguished from other plastics because it is heavier than plastic. It will also have a clunking noise when tapped rather than the lightweight clinking sound of plastic. This sound is easily heard when tapping two Bakelite bracelets together.

Bakelite can also be tested by using Simichrome Polish, which is available at most hardware stores. When a piece of Bakelite is polished with Simichrome, the cloth will have a yellow residue.

Vintage Designers

Belle Kogan

Born in Ilyashevka, Russia, Belle Kogan immigrated to the United States in 1906. While studying at the Pratt Institute and the Art Students League, she worked in her father's jewelry store. She continued her education at the Rhode Island School of Design and the Pforzheim, Germany Art School. In 1929, she worked for the Quaker Silver Company where she was trained to be a silver designer.

Ms. Kogan was the first professional female industrial designer in the United States. She opened her own office in New York, and was soon designing for many companies such as Libbey Glass, U.S. Glass, Federal Glass, Towle Manufacturing Company, Maryland Plastics, and Bakelite Corporation. From 1930-1950, she designed for Blefield & Goodfriend, jobbers for F.W. Woolworth. During this time, she created two-color jewelry, polka-dot bangles with her trademark, elongated dots.

Martha Sleeper

Martha Sleeper was an actress who channeled her creativity into a design career. She got her start making handmade jewelry from Bakelite to create whimsical and fun designs. Starting her own cottage industry, she soon turned a small sale into a larger sale to a department store, and her company grew from there. Sales eventually became so great that she could no longer make the pieces by herself and she had to hire the New England Novelty Company to manufacture her jewelry designs. Later from 1938-1942, D. Lisner manufactured her line of novelty jewelry.

Auguste Bonaz

Auguste Bonaz was a French designer who created jewelry with geometric designs. He used both Bakelite and Galalith to bring his creations to life.

Lea Stein

In 1954, Lea Stein, a French designer, began producing a whimsical line of jewelry made with multiple layers of celluloid. Ms. Stein would design the jewelry while her husband, Fernand Steinberger, would assemble the pieces. She used a process that involved laminating layers of cellulose acetate sheets together. An adhesive was then applied and baked overnight. After the material cooled, it was then cut into patterns and made into jewelry. The pins had a metal pin-back that was heat mounted and signed "Lea Stein: Paris" in block letters. She was well known for her figural pins that included foxes, cats, dogs, women, and geometric designs. Ms. Stein closed her company in 1980, but resumed production in 1991. Her new pieces can be distinguished from the older pieces by the manner in which the metal pin-backs are attached. While still signed "Lea Stein: Paris," the newer production pieces are riveted on the pin rather than being heat mounted.

Modern Designers

Judy Clarke

While visiting her friends, Ron and Ester Shultz, in 1997 and 1998, Judy Clarke tinkered around in their workshop, learning about Bakelite and working with tools. In the summer of 1999, she carved her first piece of jewelry, but she didn't begin to devote much time to it until 2001. When she first started to carve, she would only use vintage Bakelite, but she currently uses all types of thermoset plastics to create her intricately carved and designed jewelry. Each piece can take as little as 4-5 hours to create or as much as 25 hours depending upon the design. Each piece is handmade with the prep work consisting of cleaning, polishing, and buffing the surface; the carving is next, followed by the painting and decoration.

Jim Foltz

Jim Foltz first started making Bakelite jewelry in 1999. Although he does not have a design background, he did make custom jewelry and performed repairs from 1960 to 1988. Jim taught himself how to create his wonderful jewelry by trial and error. He uses poker chips, Mah-jongg racks, broken radio cases, and other Bakelite items to create a line of whimsical figurals. He starts a piece by taking a piece of material, drawing a design on it, cutting out the design with a jeweler's saw, filing it, sanding it, and then polishing it to a high finish with a buffing machine. His early designs were not signed, but after he discovered that some of his pieces were being sold as vintage, he began signing his pieces. The jewelry is available through dealers who resell his jewelry.

Clarke top and reverse-carved Lucite bangle with hand painting, glitter, and rhinestones, **$500**.

Karen and Howard Kronimus

In 1994, Karen Kronimus bought a semi truck loaded with Bakelite intending to use the applejuice cubes as beads for necklaces. But as she began going through all the raw material, her imagination took over and she began turning the Bakelite into wonderful pieces of jewelry. Her father, Howard, originally helped her by creating tools for her to use, but he soon began creating his own jewelry. The two learned by trial and error, and through the advice and guidance of other artists and manufacturers of plastics.

The first pieces that they began selling were necklaces made from Bakelite cube beads and stretch bracelets. They soon branched out from there, adding carved pieces and laminated bracelets to their line of jewelry. Each piece is signed, KK for Karen Kronimus and HK for Howard Kronimus, and is made by hand; taking from five to six hours for an inlaid piece, 12 hours for a carved piece and up to 12 hours for a laminated bracelet. The laminated bracelets are the most complicated, as each small piece of the circle must be wedge-sanded to fit the piece next to it, and to fit the bracelet's base. Then the whole bracelet is sanded to a crown shape. The Kronimus' sell their jewelry at shows and through other vintage jewelry dealers.

Ester and Ron Shultz

Ester and Ron Shultz began making Bakelite jewelry in the latter part of the 1980s. They had always sold vintage jewelry in the past, but weren't familiar with Bakelite. After a customer inquired about it, Ester began collecting Bakelite buttons. These buttons were the beginning of their foray into jewelry design. The first piece that they sold was a button necklace that went from one dealer to another all over the country. Soon dealers were begging for necklaces of their own. Their first line, necklaces made with Bakelite buttons, was an instant hit.

The Shultz' soon began designing all types of Bakelite jewelry including whimsical pins and bangles of all kinds: polka dot, checkerboard, bow tie, carved, and zigzag. The husband and wife team create the designs and then produce each piece by hand. Each piece has its own process with bangles being laminated,

sanded, and polished while pins are carved, sanded, polished, and detailed. The earliest pieces were not signed, but all pieces after this short period are signed "Shultz." In order to create these incredible designs, the Shultz' use all kinds of Bakelite items to create their jewelry including poker chips holders, Mah-jongg trays, beads, buttons, old sheets of Bakelite from 1949 juke boxes, and old stock. The jewelry is available through several dealer Web sites.

Jackie Weeks

Jackie Weeks has been a collector and dealer since she was sixteen years old. Six years ago, she turned her love of vintage jewelry and of decorating into designing and carving Bakelite jewelry. A friend had already set up a small workshop to carve Bakelite so they started working together. Two to three times a week, they would work on pieces; carving, polishing, and gluing pieces, spending hours perfecting their technique.

She uses parts and pieces of broken Bakelite as well as old stock Bakelite rods to create her designs. Each piece is designed and handmade by Weeks, who gets an idea for the design and then starts working it out in her head from beginning to end. Pieces can take from a couple of hours to make to several days to months depending upon the intricacies involved. Her favorite pieces to make are those that involve reverse carving, because she finds it a challenge to figure out what the piece will look like through a section of transparent Bakelite.

Five years ago, she started selling her designs that she usually wears. Invariably someone will purchase it off of her as she wears it. Most of her sales are custom orders, though her pieces can be purchased through vintage jewelry dealers and by contacting her directly. Her pieces are signed "MOE."

Other designers

Some other designers to note are Adrian, Judith Evans, Dan and Penny Lains, and Bruce Pantti. The jewelry of these designers can be found at Barbara B. Woods Antique Costume Jewelry at www. bwoodantique.com and at Lori Kizer's Rhinestone Airplane at www.rhinestoneairplane.com

Evans bowtie bangles, resin, **$250** *each.*

How To Collect

The first rule of collecting is to collect what you like! Don't worry about trends or what's the hot new collectible. Focus on amassing a collection that intrigues you, makes you smile, and inspires you. The possibilities are endless.

You do need to focus on the condition and the quality. Is the piece well made? Is it missing any stones or pieces? Is it cracked, chipped or scratched? Is it deteriorating? Can the piece be repaired and how much will the repair cost? These are all questions that you need to ask yourself when you are purchasing jewelry.

Condition is first and foremost. Don't overlook this. Be conscious of the condition because it will affect the value. Unless a piece is rare, or one that you truly desire, think twice before purchasing it in poor condition. If you can repair the piece yourself, or have a jeweler do it, and the price is reflective of the condition, then it might be worthwhile to purchase it. However, flaws to plastics such as cracks, chips, and scratches are often unrepairable.

The quality and the design of a piece are very important. Is it intricate and ornate? Is it handmade or machine made? How is the finish on the piece? The more detail that is involved, and the more handwork that is involved, will generally make a piece more valuable.

While age does play a role in the value of a piece, don't be fooled into believing that antique jewelry has to be over 100 years old to have any value, and that the older the piece the more valuable it is—regardless of the condition. The factor of design is a more subjective personal evaluation, more to do with your own personal taste.

Scarcity and rarity play a role in the price. Obviously, if a piece is rare and hard to find, the price will reflect it. But if a dealer has multiples of the same piece, be wary. These can be old store stock or even reproductions, and obviously, rule out the rare factor!

Remember to enjoy yourself. Part of the fun is the thrill of the hunt and finding that one piece that makes your heart stop!

Other helpful hints:

Be aware that when a piece of jewelry is a popular item, the price may be artificially high and have no bearing on the intrinsic value.

Take your time to examine the jewelry. Use a loupe to look for signatures and other marks as well as damage.

Don't buy a piece that is deteriorating.

Check for scratches, pitting, crazing, cracking, splits, nicks, warping, repairs, and glue.

Check to make sure there are no holes from heat tests.

Look for signs of age in the hardware to see if the piece is older. Generally the older pieces will use screws and rivets to secure pin-backs while the newer ones will have glued on pin-backs.

If the piece has hanging charms or beads, check the string that is attaching them.

You can run your hand over a piece to feel for cracks and nicks.

Care of Plastic Jewelry

Do not spray perfumes, deodorants or hairsprays around the jewelry. The products will adhere to the jewelry and damage them.

Be careful when handling plastic jewelry. While handling the jewelry does not cause a problem, the material can crack or break when dropped onto a hard surface.

Do not put disintegrating pieces of celluloid jewelry near other pieces of celluloid. It will cause the others to catch the "disease" and cause damage.

Celluloid should be stored in a dry place.

Do not store plastics in the direct sunlight or heat.

Store the jewelry in an area that is cool, dry and dust free.

Inspect pieces for deterioration occasionally, and if it is deteriorating, be sure to store it separately.

Do not use ammonia or ammonia-based cleaners on Lucite.

Store separately to avoid scratching, rubbing or being nicked by other pieces.

To polish, use Simichrome Polish and a soft cloth and do not over rub.

Don't use gritty or abrasive cleaners.

Do not soak celluloid or casein to clean. Use a soft cloth and gently wipe the piece.

Price Guide

The following price guide features hundreds of examples of plastic jewelry. The values in this book are only a reference point. Values vary according to each piece's condition, quality, design, and/or geographic location where the piece is purchased.

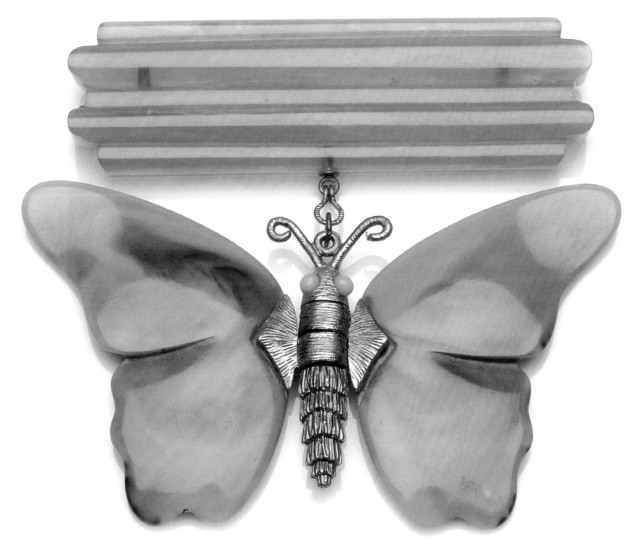

Articulated butterfly brooch, green and marbled butterscotch Bakelite, ***$1,200***.

Necklace with polka dot charms, Bakelite, **$450**.

Applejuice Bakelite, carved, hinged bangle with rhinestones, **$425**.

Applejuice Bakelite necklace, **$225**.

Bakelite pendant and chain with rhinestones, **$375**.

Cameo bracelet, Bakelite and celluloid, **$350**.

Applejuice and red Bakelite necklace, **$450**.

Red Bakelite heart brooch with green Bakelite balls, **$375**.

Carved cherry brooch, Bakelite with celluloid chain, **$750**.

*Carved Bakelite bangles, left: black, **$600**; right: butterscotch, **$500**.*

*Bakelite bangles with faux pearls, green, red, blue, topaz, and clear rhinestones, **$850** each.*

Faceted red Bakelite necklace, **$98**.

Boot brooch, Bakelite, **$145**.

Spider brooch, Bakelite and brass, **$125**.

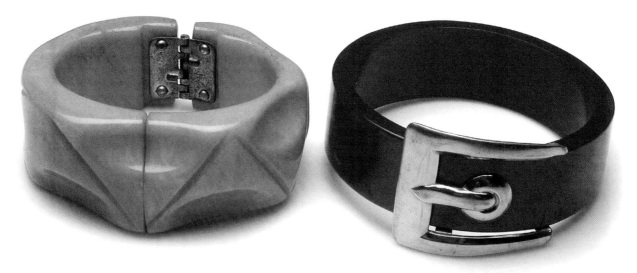

*Left: Bakelite hinged bangle, **$245**; right: red Bakelite bangle with metal buckle, **$375**.*

*Thermoplastic hinged bangle with aurora borealis rhinestones, **$225**.*

Necklace, butterscotch Bakelite, **$225**.

Articulated figural man brooch, Bakelite, **$750**.

Bird brooch, reverse-carved Lucite and wood, **$185**.

Horse brooch, butterscotch and green Bakelite with leather, **$625**.

*Left: green Bakelite dress clip, **$65**; middle: red Bakelite dress clip, **$95**; right: black Bakelite dress clip, **$95**.*

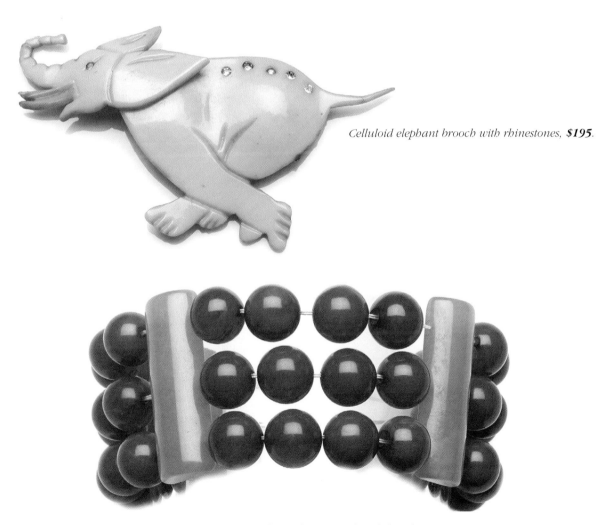

*Celluloid elephant brooch with rhinestones, **$195**.*

*Stretch bracelet on elastic, butterscotch Bakelite, **$185**.*

*Left: Lucite and red Bakelite bird brooch, **$185**; right: Lucite and green Bakelite horse brooch, **$225**.*

*Rooster brooch, celluloid with red, green, pink, aurora borealis rhinestones, **$88**.*

*Leg brooch with charms, celluloid and plastic, **$75**.*

*Fish brooch, reverse-carved Lucite and wood, **$195***.

*Flamingo brooch, Bakelite and leather, **$260***.

*Top left: reverse-carved Lucite fish brooch with hand painting, **$150**; top right: thermoset plastic fish brooch, **$65**; bottom: thermoset plastic fish brooch, **$25**.*

Horse brooch, rootbeer Bakelite, **$350**.

Indian brooch, Bakelite with rhinestones, **$1,500**.

Horse brooch with charms, Bakelite, **$750**.

Asian man figural brooch, orange Bakelite, **$225**.

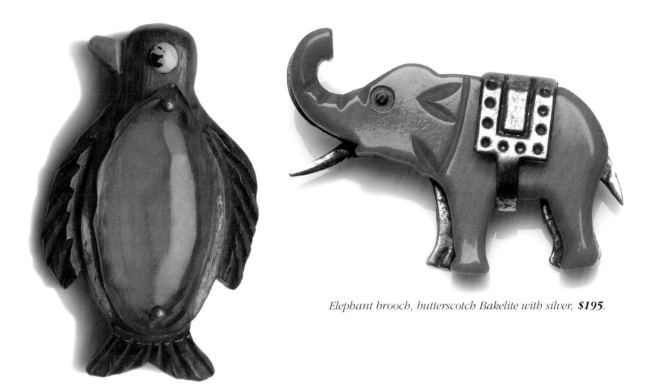

Elephant brooch, butterscotch Bakelite with silver, **$195**.

Penguin brooch, applejuice Bakelite and wood, **$395**.

Eagle brooch, black Bakelite with rhinestones, **$450**.

Turtle brooch, green Bakelite and wood, **$225**.

*Left: bangle, Lucite with embedded dried flowers, **$165**; right: faceted applejuice Bakelite bangle, **$195**.*

*Butterscotch Bakelite bangles; left stack, top to bottom: **$90** for the pair, **$150**, **$150**, **$55**; right top: **$225**; right bottom: **$175**.*

Green and black Lucite necklace, **$85**.

Hobé carved Bakelite Asian woman brooch with hand painting, **$375**.

Fish brooch, black Bakelite, **$495**.

Necklace with hard plastic flowers on celluloid chain, **$135**.

Thermoset plastic Afghan hounds brooch, **$35**.

Cowgirl brooch, plastic and wood, **$150**.

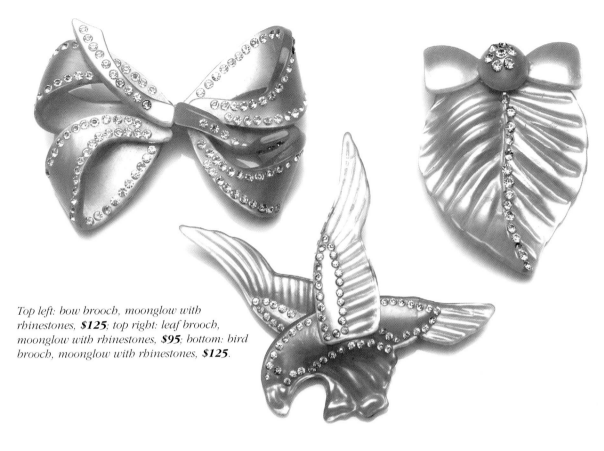

*Top left: bow brooch, moonglow with rhinestones, **$125**; top right: leaf brooch, moonglow with rhinestones, **$95**; bottom: bird brooch, moonglow with rhinestones, **$125**.*

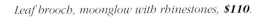

*Leaf brooch, moonglow with rhinestones, **$110**.*

*Thermoset plastic hinged bangle with aurora borealis rhinestones, **$165**.*

*Left: Kenneth Lane brooch with Lucite and rhinestones, **$395**; right: KJL turtle brooch with blue plastic body, blue cabochons, and rhinestones, **$295**.*

*Celluloid button with rhinestones, **$35**.*

*Butterfly brooch, celluloid with red, green, blue, and topaz rhinestones, **$165**.*

*Lisner necklace, earring, bracelet, and brooch set, carved Lucite
with lavender and purple rhinestones,* **$95**.

*Pin and earring set with blue moonglow cabochons
and light blue rhinestones,* **$95**.

*Hinged bangle and earring set, thermoplastic with clear and aurora borealis rhinestones, **$195**.*

*Top row: Lucite confetti earrings, from left: **$16**, **$28**, **$28**; bottom: Lucite confetti bracelet, **$65**.*

Eisenberg necklace, brooch, and earring set, thermoplastic with rhinestones, **$275**.

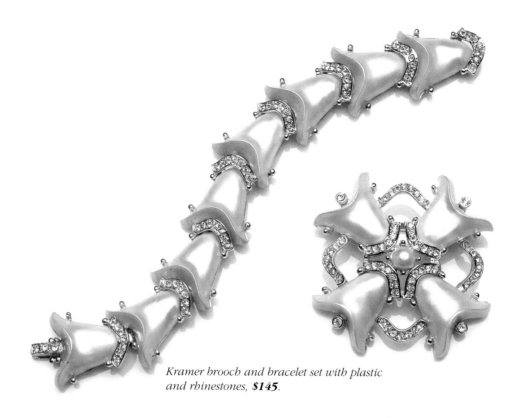

*Kramer brooch and bracelet set with plastic and rhinestones, **$145**.*

*Necklace, bracelet, and earring set, thermoset plastic with green rhinestones, **$95**.*

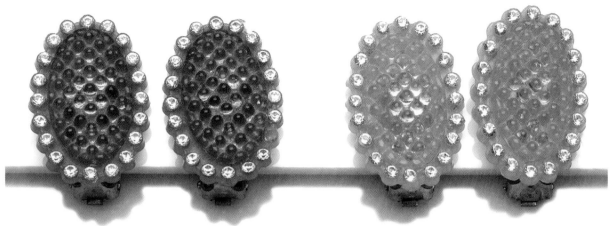

Plastic earrings with rhinestones, **$28** *each.*

Expandable bracelet and earring set, hard plastic with faux pearls, **$605**.

Molded plastic earrings with rhinestones, **$30** *each.*

Top: Occupied Japan double dog brooch, celluloid, $65;
right: Occupied Japan dog brooch, celluloid, $65.

Dog brooches, celluloid, $42 each.

Thermoset plastic flower necklace, **$80**.

Flower brooch, moonglow, **$45**.

Floral dress clip, faceted plastic and rhinestones, **$35**.

Necklace, bracelet and earring set, thermoplastic with pink and light blue rhinestones, **$325**.

Contemporary necklace and earring sets, Lucite with rhinestones, **$24** *each.*

Necklace, faceted plastic beads, **$48**.

Bracelets with confetti Lucite insets, **$65** *each.*

Trifari elephant fur clip with Lucite body, enameling, and rhinestones, **$1,900-$2,300**.

Celluloid brooch with clear, red and green rhinestones, **$225**.

Marbled green Bakelite bangle with rhinestones, **$950**.

Hinged bangle, rootbeer Bakelite, **$750**.

*Celluloid and rhinestone bangles, **$125** to **$365** each.*

*Earrings, from left: thermoset plastic with rhinestones, **$40**; Weiss thermoplastic with rhinestones, **$65**; thermoplastic with multicolored rhinestones, **$85**; thermoplastic with rhinestones, **$40**.*

*Lea Stein brooches, celluloid, from left:
contemporary flower pot $75; vintage
Edelweiss, $60.*

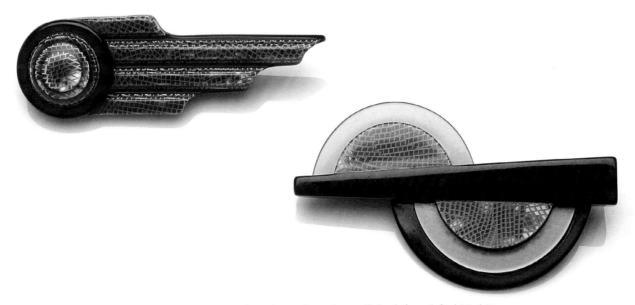

Vintage Lea Stein art-deco design brooches, celluloid, from left: $45, $48.

*Top left: flower brooch, moonglow with rhinestones, **$125**; top right: bird brooch, moonglow, **$45**; bottom: flower brooch, moonglow, **$45**.*

*Vintage Lea Stein brooches, celluloid, top: **$60**; bottom: **$58**.*

Celluloid hair comb with rhinestones, **$165**.

Celluloid hair comb with rhinestones, **$165**.

Celluloid hair comb with rhinestones, ***$125****.*

*Left: lobster brooch with plastic body, red cabochons and rhinestones, **$45**; right: lobster brooch with plastic body, faux pearls, and rhinestones, **$85**.*

*Left: fish brooch, Lucite with blue, pink, green, red, and topaz rhinestones, **$48**; right: fish brooch, Lucite with glitter, **$35**.*

Vintage Lea Stein car brooches, celluloid, **$48** *each.*

*Acorn brooch, resin finished Bakelite, **$550**.*

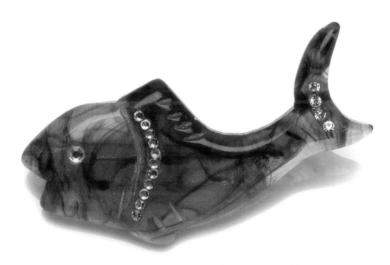

*Fish brooch, Lucite with rhinestones, **$65**.*

*Butterscotch and red Bakelite link bracelet, **$550**.*

*Left: hinged Lucite bangle with confetti and seashells, **$85**; right: Lucite confetti hinged bangle, **$65**.*

*Rootbeer and tea Bakelite bangle, **$750**.*

Brass necklace with green Bakelite leaf charms, ***$325***.

*Celluloid necklace, **$75***.

Butterscotch Bakelite earrings, **$125**.

Floral dress clips, butterscotch Bakelite, **$125** *for the pair.*

Patriotic anchor brooch, red Bakelite and plastic, **$495**.

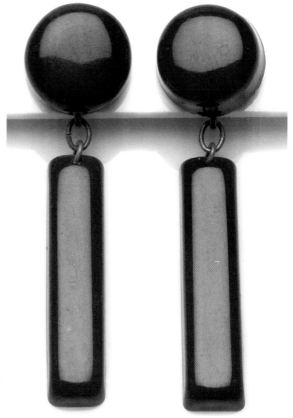

Red and blue Bakelite earrings, **$150**.

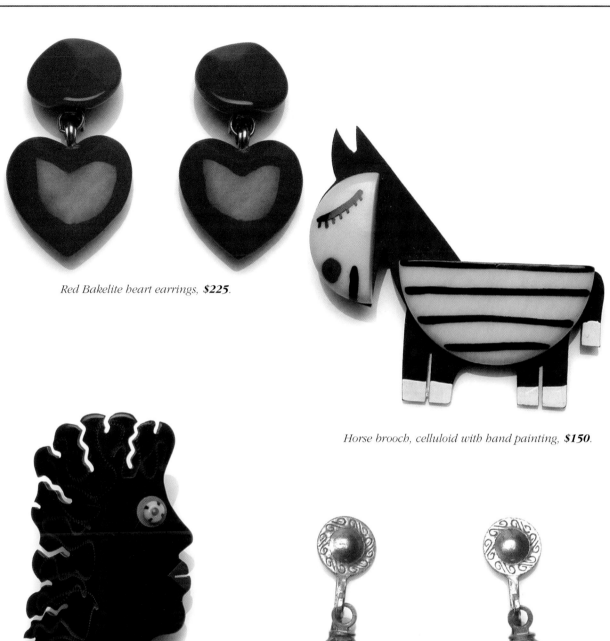

Red Bakelite heart earrings, **$225**.

Horse brooch, celluloid with hand painting, **$150**.

Lady brooch, plastic with rhinestones, **$95**.

Reverse-carved Lucite Mexican-themed earrings, **$85**.

Bakelite dot pendant on French jet beads, **$145**.

Marbled green Bakelite stretch bracelet on elastic, **$225**.

Locket on necklace, celluloid, **$195**.

Black and butterscotch Bakelite cameo brooch, **$550**.

Cameo brooch, butterscotch and applejuice Bakelite with brass, **$450**.

Cameo brooch, reverse-carved Lucite and Bakelite, **$125**.

Celluloid necklace with cameo pendant, **$245**.

Cameo pendant on chain, celluloid and Bakelite, **$195**.

Left: Cameo brooches, left: red Bakelite, **$275**;
right: butterscotch and black Bakelite, **$225**.

Reverse-carved Lucite woman design necklace and earring set, **$85**.

*Cameo brooches, from left: Bakelite with reverse-carved Lucite, **$145**;
right: Bakelite with Lucite, **$95**.*

*Cameo brooches, from left: plastic and Lucite, **$75**; thermoset plastic in silver frame, **$125**;
right: hard plastic, **$35**.*

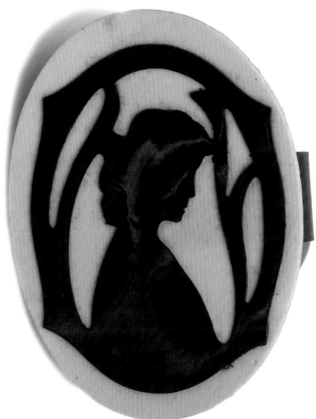

*Woman in silhouette belt buckle, celluloid, **$145**.*

Flower necklace, celluloid, **$65**.

*Carved Bakelite bangles with aluminum, **$550** each.*

*Carved and pierced Bakelite bangles, from left: black, burnt orange, cream corn, and marbled mocha, **$225** each.*

Polka-dot bangles, Bakelite, **$275** *each.*

Vendome necklace and earring set, Lucite beads with faceted glass beads, **$65**.

Heart brooches, thermoset plastic, from left: **$45**, **$35**, **$35**, **$35**.

Heart brooches, thermoset plastic, from left: **$55**, **$45**, **$35**.

Bangle with front section made up of individual pieces strung on elastic, Bakelite, $750.

Prystal bangles with carving and rhinestones, $450 each.

Heart brooch with dangling balls, Bakelite, **$325**.

Flower brooches, faceted plastic with faux pearls and brass,
$42 *for the pair.*

Fruit earrings, plastic, **$45** *each.*

Celluloid locket with photograph on celluloid chain, **$185**.

Dog in ship wheel brooch on original card, hard plastic, **$65**.

Flower brooch with thermoset plastic, **$38**.

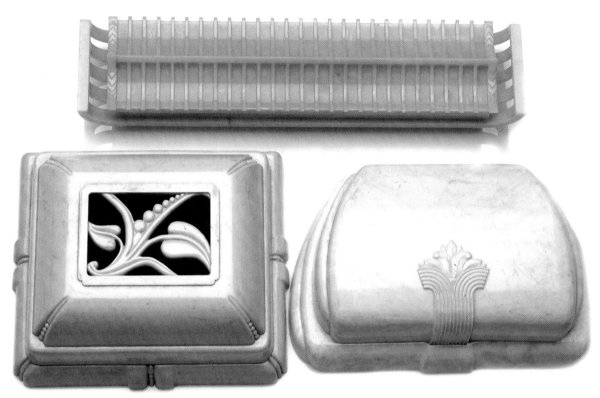

Jewelry boxes, thermoset plastic, clockwise from top: **$35**, **$30**, **$35**.

*Reverse zigzag Bakelite bangles, from left: bright green/light blue green,
corn/chocolate, green/light khaki green,* **$375** *each.*

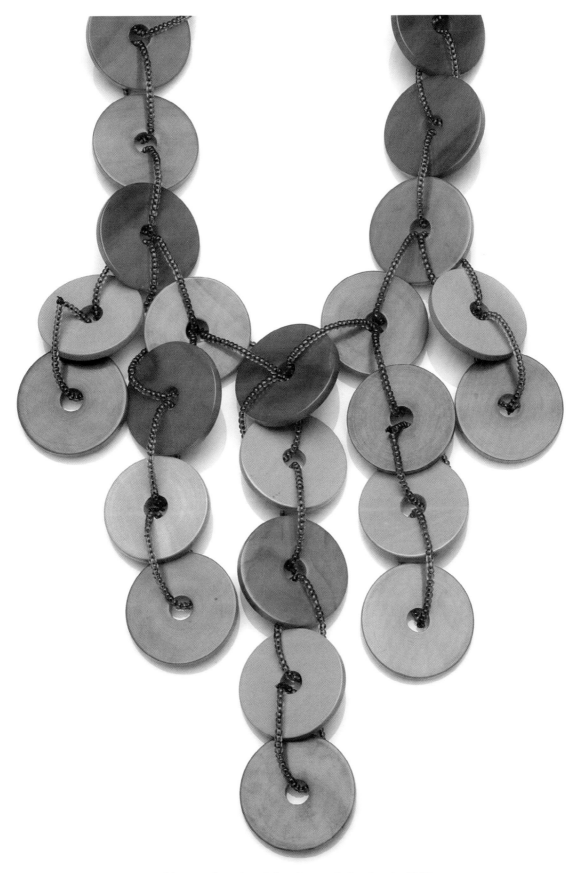

Necklace made with Bakelite discs and glass beads, **$345**.

Green Bakelite and plastic figural brooch, **$195**.

Top left: Bakelite ring, **$95**; *top right: marbled green and butterscotch Bakelite ring,* **$145**; *bottom: marbled green Bakelite ring,* **$95**.

Marbled green Bakelite earrings with metal accents, **$125**.

Dice brooch, Bakelite, **$225**.

*Top: Lucite bangle, **$35**; bottom left: Bakelite bangle, **$275**; bottom right: hard plastic bangle, **$85**.*

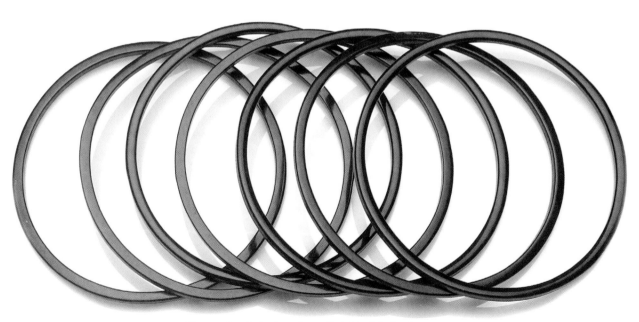

*Vintage Lea Stein bangles, celluloid, **$70** for the set.*

Dice necklace, hard plastic, **$325**.

*Art deco celluloid belt with metal accents, **$185**.*

*Left: clown brooch, Bakelite on wood, **$275**;*
*right: pair of owl brooches, galalith, **$225**.*

*Left: chrome and end-of-day Bakelite brooch, **$165**;*
*right: chrome and green Bakelite brooch, **$125**.*

*Vendome flower brooch with plastic flowers,
rhinestones, and glass beads,* **$55**.

Plastic fruit design pin and earring set, **$45**.

*Left: Googly-eye mouse brooch, Lucite, **$300**;*
*right: Googly-eye owl brooch, Lucite, **$300**.*

*Cat brooch, Bakelite, **$295**.*

End-of-day carved Bakelite bangles, left: black, orange, butterscotch, and yellow, $600; right: light green, brown, orange, and yellow, $550.

Top left: Asian-design brooch with thermoplastic and black rhinestones, $95; top right and bottom: Asian-design earrings and matching bracelet, thermoplastic with faux pearls and green rhinestones, $85.

Alice Caviness necklace and earring set, faceted plastic beads with faceted glass beads, red, orange, and lavender rhinestones, $345.

Celluloid bangle and earring set with rhinestones, **$225**.

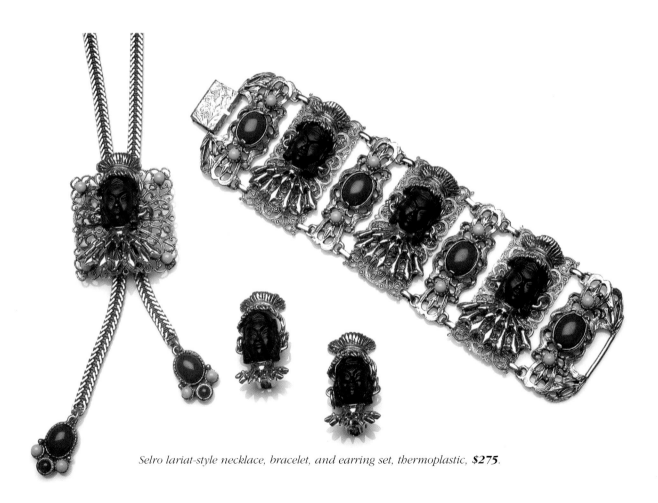

Selro lariat-style necklace, bracelet, and earring set, thermoplastic, **$275**.

Har brooch, earring, and bracelet set, thermoplastic with red, aurora borealis rhinestones, **$1,400**.

Hobé necklace, bracelet, and earrings with plastic fruit and beads, ***$195****.*

Carved Bakelite bangles, from left: marbled green, red, and black, **$395** *each.*

Fruit brooch and earring set, Lucite with orange rhinestones and enameling, **$110***.*

Flower brooch with Lucite petals and red rhinestones, **$125***.*

*Left: celluloid bangle with lavender and clear rhinestones, **$85**; middle: carved Bakelite bangle with rhinestones, **$150**; right: celluloid snake bangle with blue rhinestones, **$185**.*

*Carved and over-dyed Bakelite bangles, **$285** each.*

Necklace and earring set, thermoplastic hoops, **$265**.

Thermoplastic earrings with rhinestones, **$12** *each.*

*Celluloid and applejuice Bakelite necklace, **$325***.

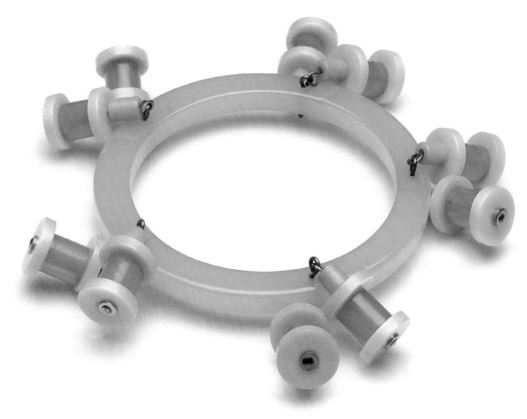

Lime green Bakelite bangle with spool charms, **$195**.

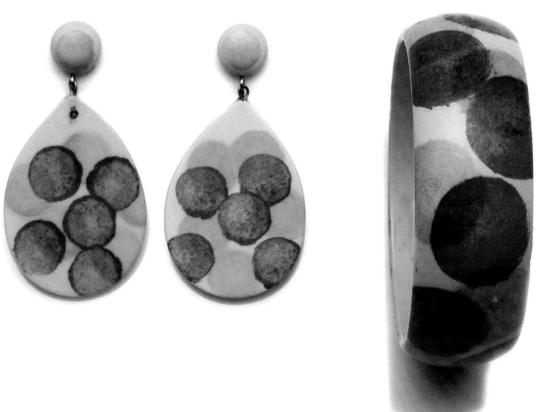

Bangle and earring set, yellow Bakelite with sponge-painted dots, **$225**.

*Left: heart charm, Lucite with metal cross, **$45**; middle: heart charm, Lucite with metal leaf, **$30**; right: heart charm, Lucite with metal military insignia, **$85**.*

*Bracelet and earring set with faceted plastic and metal beads, **$155**.*

Celluloid and thermoplastic necklace and bracelet set, ***$195***.

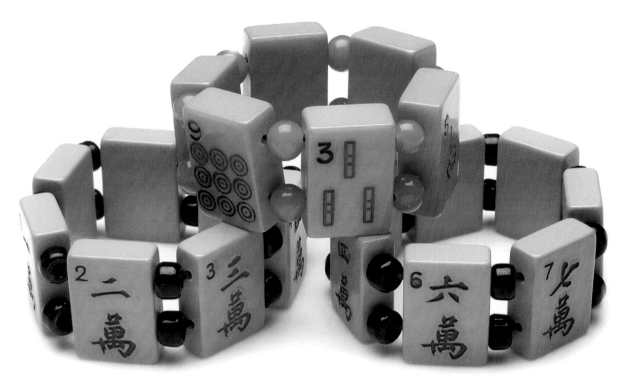

*Mah-jongg tile elastic stretch bracelets, Bakelite, **$95** each.*

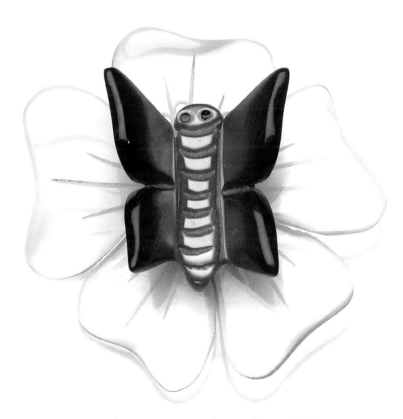

*Butterfly on reverse-carved Lucite flower, **$175**.*

*Left: marbled butterscotch Bakelite earrings, **$40**; right: marbled Bakelite earrings, **$35**.*

*Top left: carved butterscotch Bakelite earrings, **$38**; top middle: marbled butterscotch Bakelite earrings, **$32**;
top right: marbled butterscotch Bakelite earrings with brass, **$65**; bottom: marbled butterscotch Bakelite earrings, **$55**.*

*Sword brooches, Bakelite with metal accents, **$525** each.*

*Horse design stretch bracelet on elastic, butterscotch Bakelite, **$950**.*

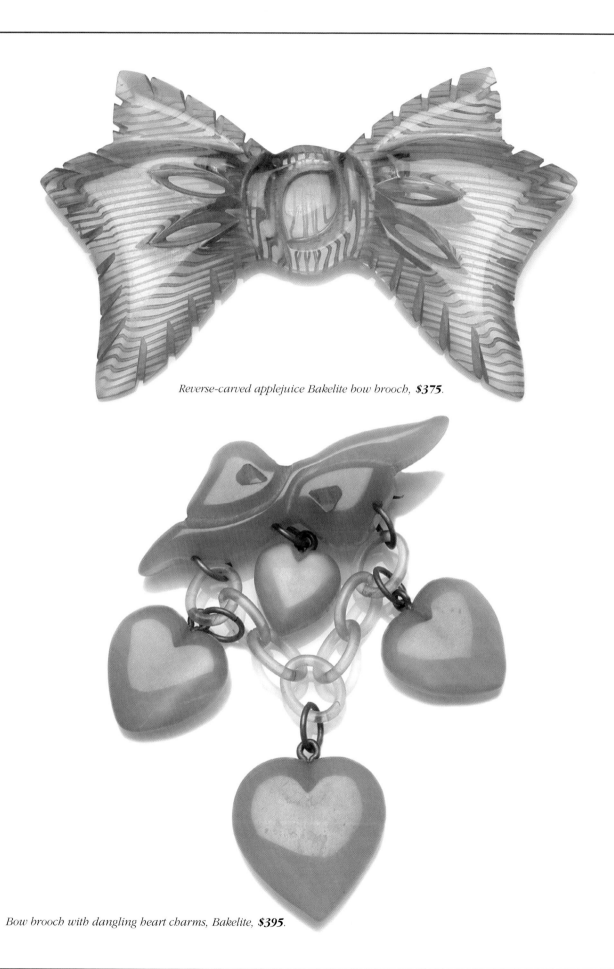

Reverse-carved applejuice Bakelite bow brooch, **$375***.*

Bow brooch with dangling heart charms, Bakelite, **$395***.*

Photo button, celluloid, ***$95****.*

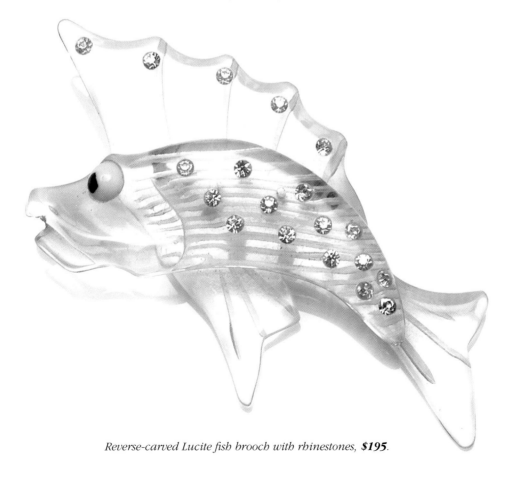

Reverse-carved Lucite fish brooch with rhinestones, ***$195****.*

Lucite cuff, **$125**.

Horse brooch, reverse-carved Lucite, **$195**.

Translucent marbled cinnamon Bakelite bangle with charms, **$195**.

Bracelet and earring set, butterscotch Bakelite, **$295**.

Marbled blue Bakelite bangle, **$350**.

Hattie Carnegie necklace and earring set with carved thermoplastic, **$265**.

*Thermoset plastic earrings with rhinestones, Western Germany; **$16** each.*

*Left: celluloid earrings with pink rhinestones, **$65**; middle: thermoplastic earrings with pink, light blue, green, and citrine rhinestones, **$85**; right: celluloid earrings with green rhinestones, **$65**.*

*Left: thermoset plastic earrings with rhinestones, Western Germany, **$16**; middle: earrings with moonglow thermoplastic cabochons, plastic leaves, and aurora borealis rhinestones, **$35**; right: thermoset plastic earrings with light blue rhinestones, **$28**.*

Art deco necklace, Galalith, **$150**.

*Necklace and earring set, molded plastic, **$95**.*

*Left: celluloid earrings with rhinestones, **$85**; right: Bakelite earrings with rhinestones, **$65**.*

*Thermoplastic hinged bangles with rhinestones, **$185** each.*

Flower brooch, reverse carved Lucite and wood, **$150**.

Fish pendant, Lucite with rhinestone eye, **$65**.

Hair pins, Lucite with glitter stars, **$45** *for the pair.*

*Kenneth Lane thermoplastic hinged bangle with rhinestones, **$275**.*

*Art deco bracelet, Bakelite and sterling, **$225**.*

Laminated bangle, applejuice and butterscotch Bakelite, **$650**.

Top: green and corn marbled Bakelite bangle, **$125**;
bottom: marbled green Bakelite bangles, **$125** *each*.

Flower brooch, black Bakelite, $500.

Bar pin with dangling charms on celluloid chain, black Bakelite, $475.

Floral design brooch, black Bakelite, $475.

*Military brooch with hanging drums and matching earrings, Bakelite, **$850**.*

*Ribbon brooch, black, green, and butterscotch marbled Bakelite, **$395**.*

*Frog riding an alligator brooch, Bakelite and wood, **$1,100**.*

Green and yellow marbled Bakelite hinged bangle with brass accents, **$250**.

Top: Bakelite bangle, **$125***; bottom left: Bakelite bangle,* **$225***;
bottom right: Bakelite bangle,* **$275**.

Floral bracelet with metal and plastic flowers and rhinestones, ***$110***.

Celluloid and rhinestone bangles, ***$95*** *to* ***$275*** *each.*

Link bracelet, red Bakelite, ***$345***.

*Floral dress clip with carved Lucite leaves, glass beads, and rhinestones, **$425**.*

*Reverse carved Lucite brooch with dangling plastic flowers, **$295**.*

*H. Pomerantz flower dress clip, thermoset plastic, **$42**.*

*Top: dress clip, celluloid with rhinestones, **$42**; bottom: art deco pin, celluloid with rhinestones, **$40**.*

*Vintage Lea Stein brooches, celluloid; left: butterfly, **$55**; right: leaf, **$50**.*

*Left: bug brooch, celluloid with rhinestones, **$165**; right: art deco design, celluloid with rhinestones, **$85**.*

*Plastic earrings with rhinestones, **$26** each.*

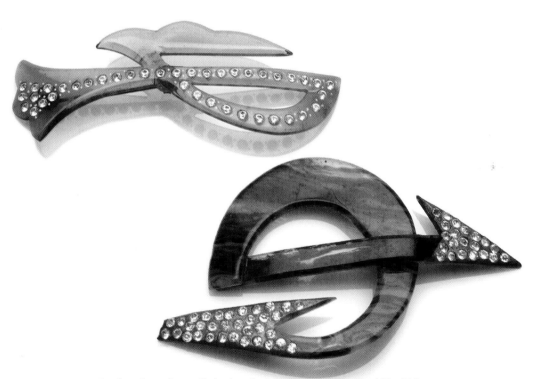

*Art deco brooches, celluloid with rhinestones, from left: **$62**, **$75**.*

Hinged bangle with matching earrings, confetti Lucite, ***$110***.

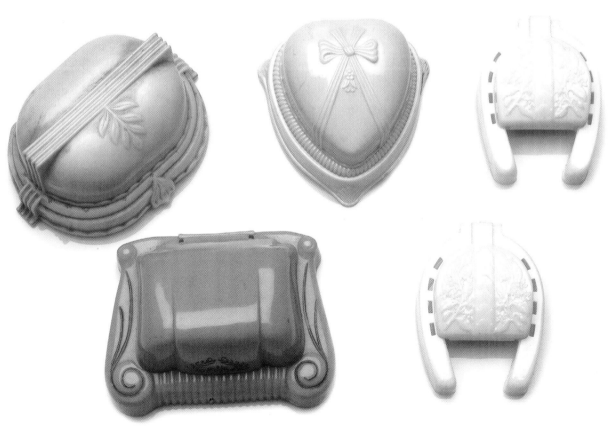

Ring boxes, top left: thermoplastic, ***$65***; *top middle: thermoset plastic,* ***$65***; *top and bottom right: thermoset plastic,* ***$35*** *each; bottom left: thermoplastic,* ***$65***.

Necklace, celluloid chain and Bakelite beads, **$45**.

Carved Lucite frog brooch, reverse-carved Lucite lily pad, ***$175****.*

Brooch with intaglio of ship and water, Bakelite, ***$235****.*

Reverse-carved Lucite palm tree brooch, ***$60****.*

Reverse-carved Lucite brooch, ***$65****.*

Rooster brooch, Bakelite, ***$210****.*

Dog brooch, reverse-carved Lucite, ***$225****.*

Left: pig brooch with leather ear, galalith, ***$150****;*
right: leaf brooch, galalith and wood, ***$95****.*

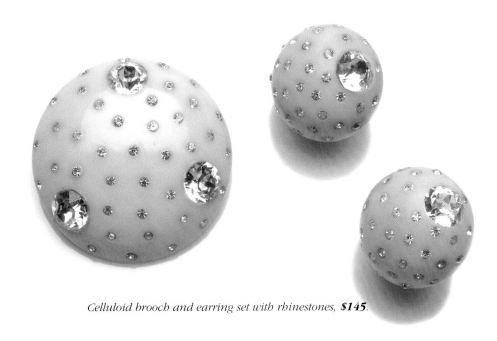

Celluloid brooch and earring set with rhinestones, **$145**.

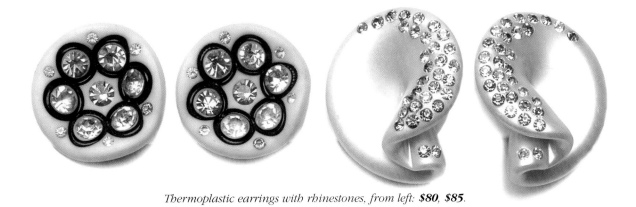

Thermoplastic earrings with rhinestones, from left: **$80**, **$85**.

Lucite bangle with gold metal accents and rhinestones, **$115**.

Lucite bangles, **$25** *each.*

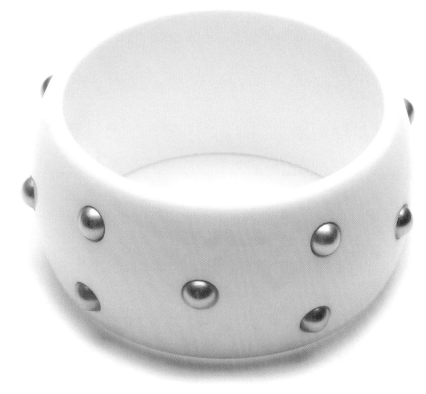

*Studded white Lucite bangle, **$38**.*

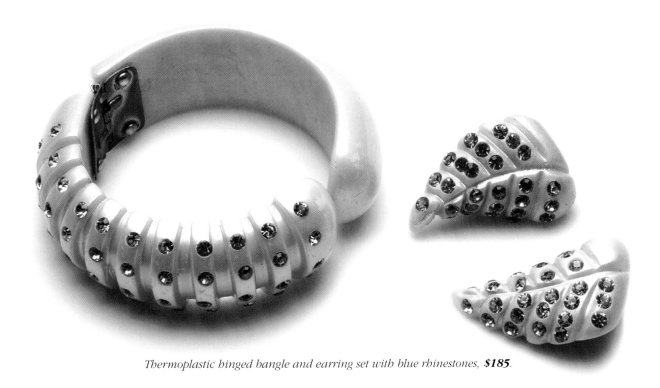

*Thermoplastic hinged bangle and earring set with blue rhinestones, **$185**.*

Plastic earrings with faux pearls and rhinestones, **$28**.

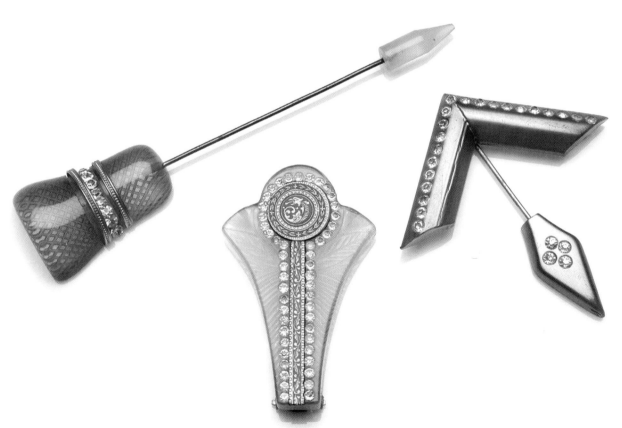

Left: celluloid hatpin with rhinestones, **$110***; middle: art deco celluloid brooch with rhinestones,* **$95***;
right: art deco celluloid brooch with rhinestones,* **$110**.

*Bakelite bangles, from left: **$275**, **$150**, **$295**.*

*Bakelite stretch bracelet with silver metal spacers and rhinestones, **$475**.*

Buckle, black Bakelite with silver, **$95**.

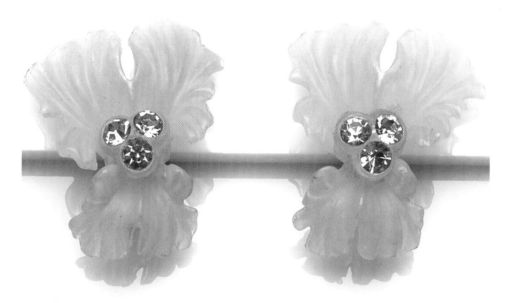

Flower earrings, Lucite with rhinestones, **$2-$5**.

Marbled Bakelite necklace, **$145**.

*Top-carved and reverse-carved and painted applejuice Bakelite and black Bakelite brooch, **$550**.*

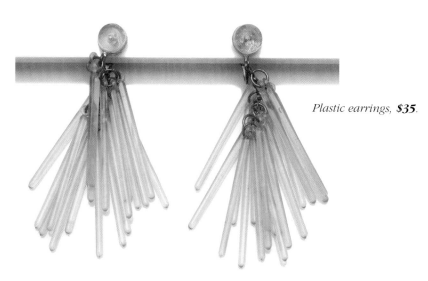

*Plastic earrings, **$35**.*

*Top: Lucite bangle, **$45**; bottom left: hard plastic bangle, **$42**; bottom right: hard plastic bangle, **$45**.*

KJL elephant pendant with Bakelite horn, **$145***.*

Brooch and earring set, Bakelite with M and M dots, **$450***.*

Celluloid necklace, **$65**.

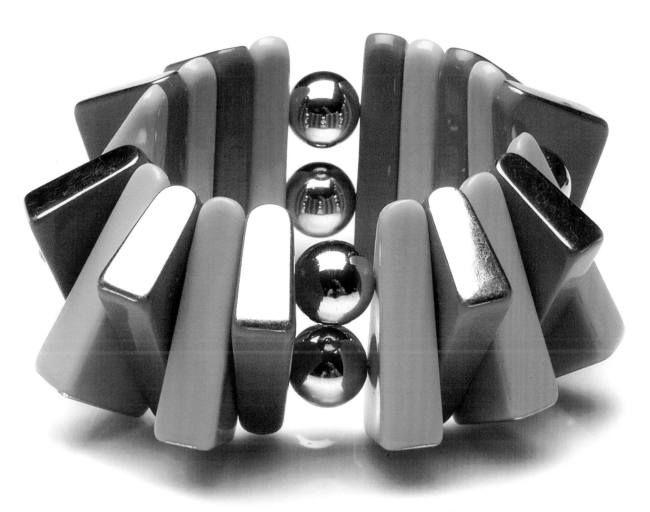

Hard plastic stretch bracelet on elastic with beads, **$65**.

Schnauzer brooch, thermoset plastic, **$65**.

Pineapple brooch, tortoiseshell, **$145**.

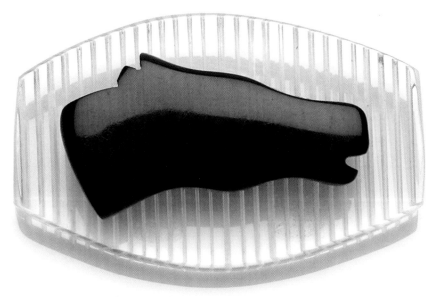

Horse brooch, Bakelite with reverse-carved Lucite, **$185**.

Bow necklace, carved Bakelite on French jet beads, $95.

Bakelite brooch with rhinestones, $165.

Crib toy necklace, Bakelite, celluloid and hard plastic, **$135**.

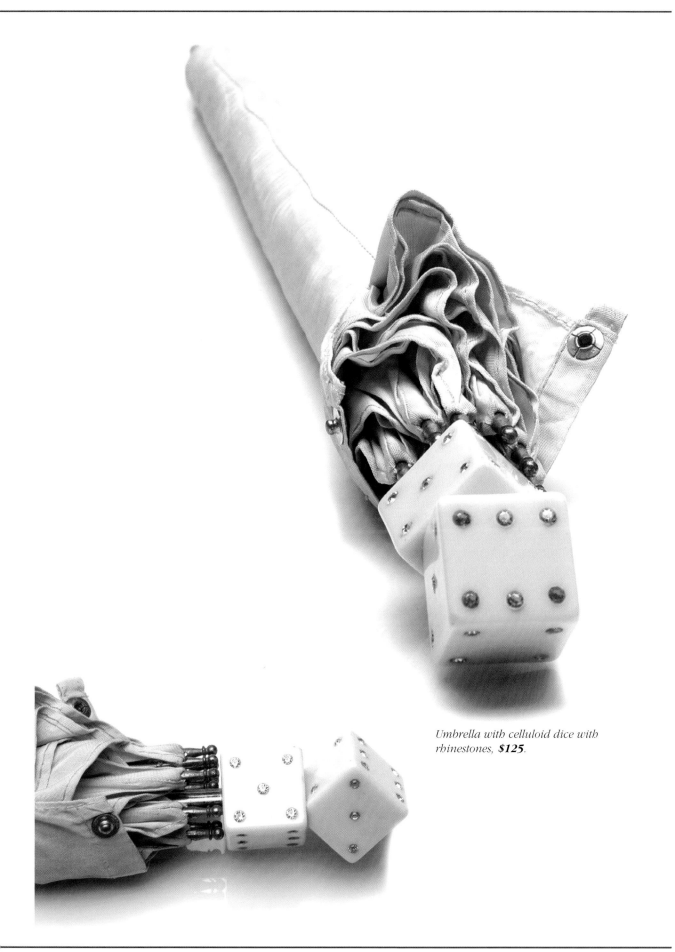

*Umbrella with celluloid dice with rhinestones, **$125**.*

Carved Bakelite earrings, **$125**.

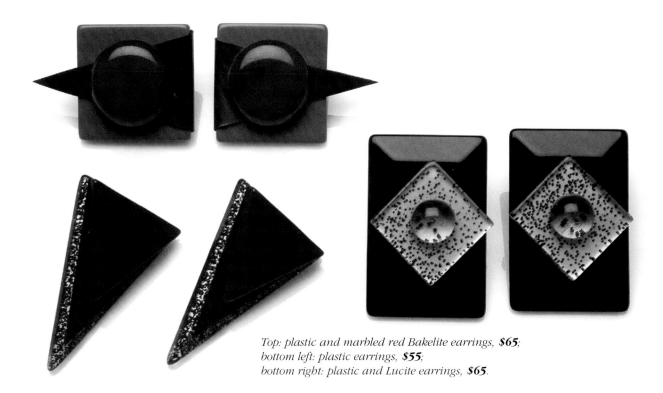

Top: plastic and marbled red Bakelite earrings, **$65**;
bottom left: plastic earrings, **$55**;
bottom right: plastic and Lucite earrings, **$65**.

Carved Bakelite bangle, **$325**.

Rope carved stretch bracelet on metal, Bakelite, **$185**.

*Left: cream corn Bakelite bangle with sponge-painted dots, **$165**;
middle: carved cream corn Bakelite bangle with hand painting, **$450**;
right: red Bakelite bangle with hand painting, **$150**.*

*Zigzag bangles, Bakelite, **$750** each.*

*Left: plastic dog brooch, **$65**; middle: red plastic dog brooch, **$55**; right: plastic Native American riding horse brooch, **$45**.*

*Left: art deco dress clip with red Bakelite and rhinestones, **$165**; middle: green and butterscotch Bakelite dress clip, **$155**; right: red Bakelite dress clip with red and clear rhinestones, **$125**.*

Celluloid dress clip, **$65**.

Top: horse earrings, Bakelite, **$225**; *bottom: horse brooch with brass accents,* **$450**.

Left: carved and tinted Lucite turtle brooch, **$160**;
right: Lucite horse brooch with hand painting, **$175**.

Cactus earrings, hard plastic with rhinestones, **$65**.

Left: sterling vermeil fish brooch with carved Lucite belly, **$495**;
*right: sterling vermeil rabbit brooch with Lucite belly and clear
and red rhinestones,* **$295**.

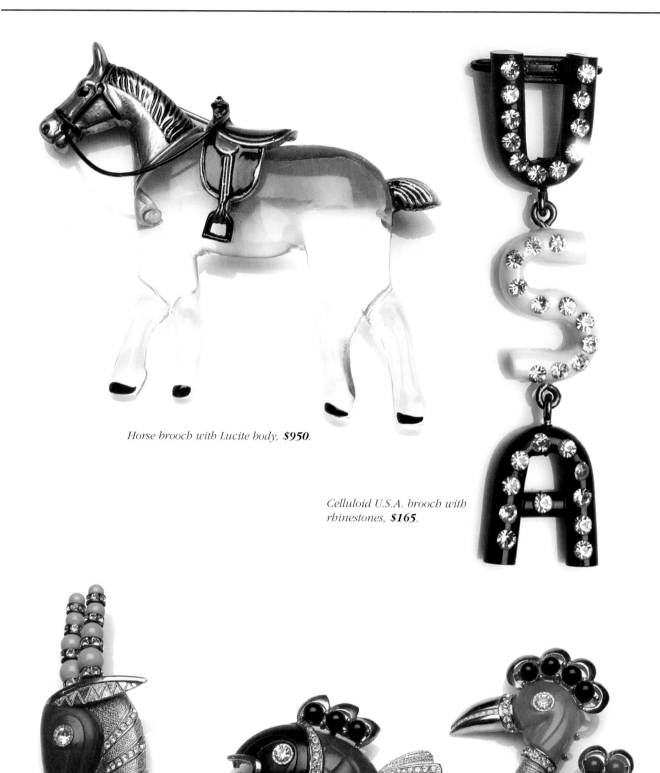

Horse brooch with Lucite body, $950.

Celluloid U.S.A. brooch with rhinestones, $165.

Hattie Carnegie brooches with plastic bodies, beads, and rhinestones; from left: $145, $130, $130.

*Thermoplastic necklace with brass, **$145***.

Lucite reverse-carved flower brooch, **$35**.

Celluloid brooch, **$68**.

Mother brooch, celluloid, **$22**.

Bird brooch with red Bakelite and wood, **$225**.

Rootbeer Lucite horse brooch, **$145**.

Selro bracelet, thermoplastic charms with lavender rhinestones, **$245**.

*Carved hinged bangle, butterscotch Bakelite, **$350**.*

*Left: corn Bakelite bangle, **$265**; right: butterscotch bangle, **$250**.*

*Celluloid pendant and chain with paint and blue
and clear rhinestones,* **$325**.

Nautical brooch, butterscotch
Bakelite and wood, **$350**.

Occupied Japan flower basket brooch, celluloid, **$55**.

Necklace, green Bakelite and brass, **$395**.

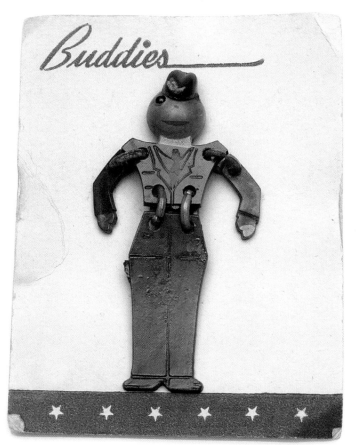

Military "Buddies" brooch on original card, plastic, $245.

Laminated Lucite rings, $20 each.

*Gemtone hand-carved flower brooch and earring set, Lucite, **$50**.*

*Left: Bug brooch, nylon, **$150**; middle: Parrot brooch, polyester with hand painting, **$95**; right: owl brooch, nylon with hand painting, **$75**.*

Plastic novelty pins on original cards,
$20 *each.*

Octagonal-shaped Lucite bangle with real bugs inside, ***$275***.

Double dog brooch, thermoset plastic with green and yellow rhinestones, $45.

Hinged bangle with matching earrings, black thermoplastic with topaz rhinestones, $245.

*Celluloid brooch with rhinestones, **$125**.*

*Fish brooch, reverse-carved Lucite with hand painting and wood, **$195**.*

*Left: horse brooch, Lucite and wood, **$95**; right: bird brooch, reverse-carved Lucite and wood, **$125**.*

Dog brooch, Lucite and wood, **$175**.

Googly-eye horse brooch, Bakelite, **$850**.

Bracelet with marbled green Bakelite beads and brass, **$350**.

Bakelite bangle, ***$950****.*

Man in sombrero pin, celluloid with hand-painting, ***$65****.*

Horse brooch, Lucite with wood, ***$185****.*

Carved bangle, chocolate Bakelite, **$850**.

Left: celluloid bangle with rhinestones, **$36***; middle: celluloid bangle with rhinestones,* **$165**.
Right: thermoplastic hinged bangle with rhinestones and hand painting, **$185**.

*Contemporary Italian stretch bracelet on elastic, Lucite, **$125**.*

*Contemporary hard plastic cuffs with rhinestones, **$36** each.*

*Native American design brooch, celluloid with leather, **$45**.*

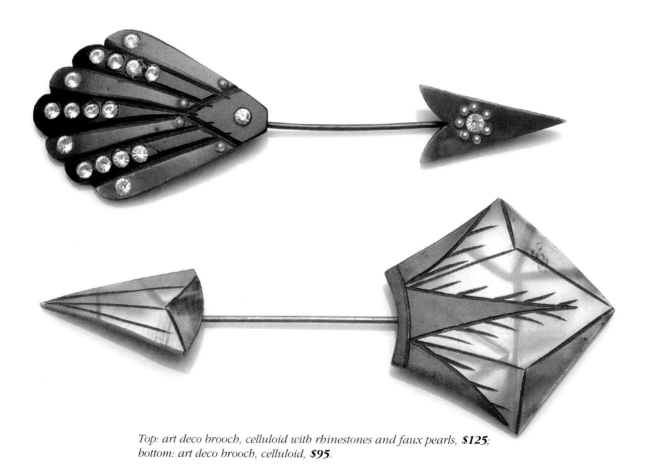

*Top: art deco brooch, celluloid with rhinestones and faux pearls, **$125**;
bottom: art deco brooch, celluloid, **$95**.*

Contemporary Lucite cuffs with applied designs, **$12** *each.*

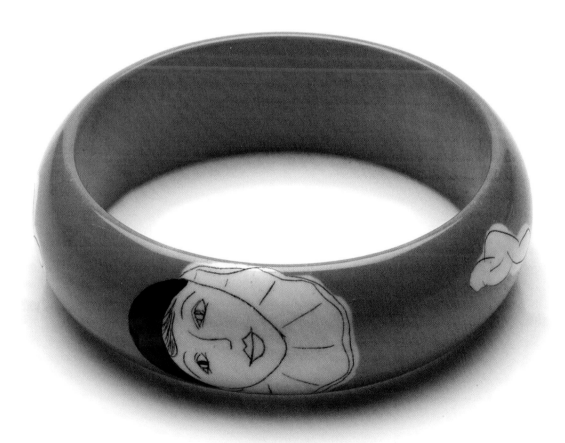

Butler and Wilson Galalith bangle, **$500**.

Bird brooch, confetti Lucite, **$95**.

Left: green Bakelite bangle, **$250**; *right: burnt orange Bakelite bangle,* **$450**.

Bakelite and celluloid brooch, **$175**.

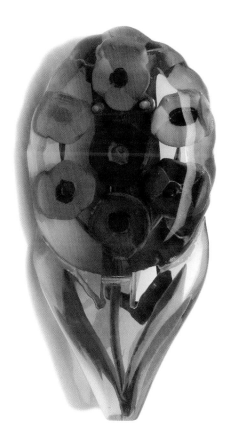

Reverse-carved painted applejuice Bakelite dress clip, **$195**.

*Lucite pendant with embedded dried flowers, **$25**.*

*Left: Hattie Carnegie clown brooch with thermoplastic face, enameling, and rhinestones, **$345**; right: Hattie Carnegie brooch with thermoplastic face, glass beads, and rhinestones, **$365**.*

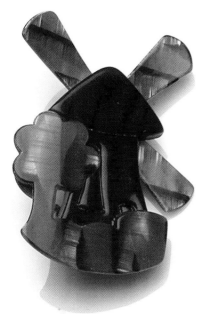

*Vintage Lea Stein brooches, celluloid, left: windmill, **$48**; right: book, **$45**.*

*Hockey sticks and skates pin, thermoset plastic, **$36**.*

Sailor brooch, celluloid, **$95**.

Kiss Timer brooch with moving hourglass, plastic, **$85**.

*Marbled Bakelite bangles, **$125** each.*

*Faceted Bakelite bangles, top left and top right: green, **$135** for the pair;*
*top middle: amber with swirls, **$65**; bottom left: red, **$175**;*
*bottom middle: black, **$95**; bottom right: mahogany brown, **$135**.*

*Six polka-dot bangles, Bakelite, **$750** each.*

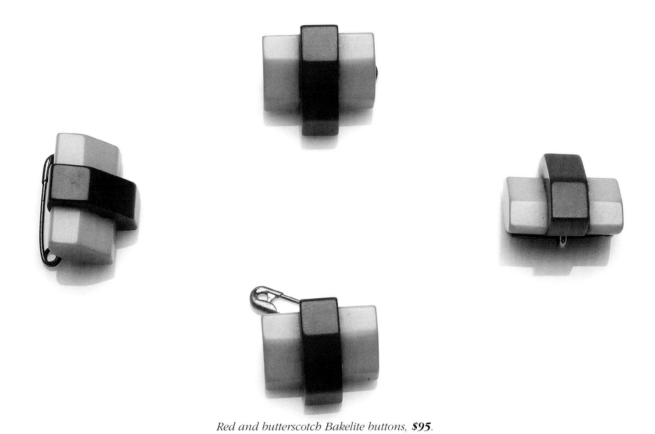

Red and butterscotch Bakelite buttons, **$95**.

Left: Lucite bangle with rhinestones, **$48**;
right: snake bangle, reverse-carved painted Lucite, damage to the tail, **$48**.

Carved brooch, green Bakelite, **$425**.

Dragon brooch, Bakelite, **$950**.

Flower brooch, green and butterscotch marbled Bakelite, **$395**.

Black Bakelite bow brooch, **$675**.

Scottie dog brooch, Bakelite, **$225**.

Left: celluloid heart brooch with rhinestones, **$125**;
right: celluloid moth brooch with rhinestones, **$125**.

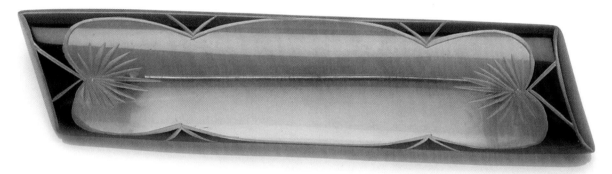

Reverse-carved applejuice and black Bakelite brooch, **$550**.

Left: Shultz bangle, Bakelite, **$1,800**; *middle: multicolored bowtie bangle, Bakelite,* **$1,600**; *right: polka-dot bangle, green and corn Bakelite,* **$1,900**.

Bakelite fruit basket brooch, **$475**.

Acorn brooch with Bakelite and wood, **$425**.

Reverse-carved applejuice Bakelite flower brooch, ***$125***.

*Egyptian Revival cameo brooch, applejuice
Bakelite with celluloid cameo,* ***$195***.

Bakelite bangles, from left: **$125**, **$165**, **$125**.

Carved Bakelite bangles, left and right: wine over-dyed; middle: pale green over-dyed, **$400** *for the set.*

Reverse-carved Lucite rooster cufflinks, **$65**.

Green Bakelite brooch with metal floral accents, **$185**.

*Cat brooches, Bakelite and brass, Czechoslovakian, **$175** each.*

*Left: carved butterscotch Bakelite stretch bracelet on elastic, **$295**; middle: butterscotch Bakelite bangle, **$125**; right red rope-carved Bakelite bangle, Bakelite, **$100**.*

*Bangles, from left: polka dot, marbled blue Bakelite, **$850**; six polka dot, marbled green Bakelite, **$800**; Belle Kogan elongated dots, Bakelite, **$1,800+** each.*

Celluloid bracelet with Bakelite charms, **$225**.

Reverse-carved Lucite flower earrings, **$45**.

Gemtone hand-carved flower pin and earring sets, **$50** *each.*

Left: celluloid and rhinestone bangle, **$265**;
right: celluloid and rhinestone bangle, **$195**.

*Earrings, left: Bakelite, **$85**; right: Bakelite, **$30**.*

*Thermoplastic earrings with aurora borealis rhinestones, **$65**.*

*Bakelite earrings, from left: **$30**, **$45**.*

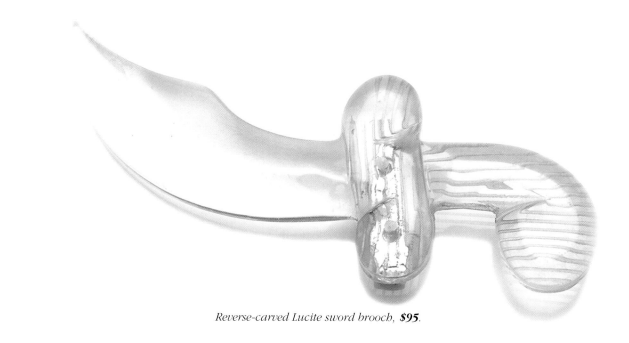

Reverse-carved Lucite sword brooch, **$95**.

Butterscotch Bakelite earrings, **$65**.

Occupied Japan Snow White brooch, celluloid, **$95**.

Fish brooch, Lucite and ceramic, ***$195***.

Frog brooch, reverse-carved Lucite and wood, ***$175***.

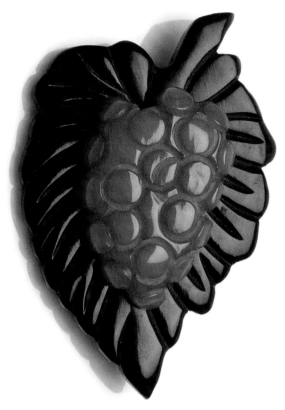

Leaf brooch, butterscotch and black Bakelite, **$500**.

Perfume pot brooch, black Bakelite, **$275**.

*Rope carved bangles, Bakelite, **$225** for the pair.*

*Bottom: Bakelite bangle with rhinestones, **$95**;*
*top: double snake bangle, celluloid with rhinestones, **$325**.*

Reverse-carved Lucite flower brooch, **$40**.

Top left: Flower brooch, Bakelite, **$325***;*
bottom left: butterfly buckle, Bakelite, **$85***;*
right: flower brooch, Bakelite, **$625**.

Plastic dog pin, **$42**.

Plastic flower brooch, **$55**.

Plastic dog pins, from left: **$48**, **$42**.

Lucite butterfly brooch with hand-painting, **$135**.

*Top: two-tone Bakelite bangle, **$265**;*
*second: carved butterscotch Bakelite bangle: **$150**;*
*third: carved butterscotch Bakelite bangle, **$150**;*
*bottom: carved butterscotch bangle, **$250**.*

*Celluloid floral design bangle, hand-painted, **$85** each.*

*Bakelite bangle with Scottie dogs, **$325**.*

*Left: carved Bakelite bangle, **$125**; middle: stretch Bakelite bracelet, **$175**;
right: faceted green Bakelite bangle, **$175**.*

Celluloid necklace with celluloid charms, **$325**.

*Far left: Lucite lipstick holder with embedded flower, **$36**;
second left; Lucite lipstick holder with embedded flower, **$36**;
third left: Lucite ring holder with embedded flower, **$42**;
right: lipstick holder with embedded flower, **$36**.*

*Celluloid snake bangles with rhinestones, left: **$185**; middle:**$185**; right: **$225**.*

Carved red Bakelite bangles, top: **$325**; *middle:* **$275**; *bottom:* **$175**.

*Celluloid floral bangles, left: **$75**; right: **$65**.*

*Celluloid bangles, left: **$65**; second left: **$65**;*
*middle: **$85**; second right: **$85**; right: **$85**.*

*Celluloid bangles with rhinestones, left: **$36**; right: **$325**.*

*Celluloid snake bangles with rhinestones, left: **$325**; right: **$325**.*

Celluloid floral design bangles, **$85** *each.*

Pearlized plastic bangles, floral design, **$65** *each.*

*Left: carved celluloid bangle with hand-painting, **$295**;*
*middle: carved celluloid snake bangle with hand-painting and rhinestones, **$325**;*
*right: carved celluloid bangle with hand-painting, **$345**.*

*Celluloid dog brooch, **$65**.*

Art deco celluloid pendant with topaz and red rhinestones, some wear, **$125**.

Necklace with applejuice Bakelite beads, ***$195****.*

Top: plastic dog brooch with moveable heads, **$65**;
bottom left: plastic double dog pin connected by chain, **$65**;
bottom right: plastic double dog pin, **$36**.

Left: plastic dog brooch, **$65**; right: plastic dog brooch, **$40**.

Contemporary Lucite bangles with rhinestones, **$24** *each.*

Contemporary Lucite cuffs with rhinestones, **$15** *each.*

Contemporary hard plastic bangles with rhinestones, **$24** *each.*

Modern Designers

Evans checkerboard bangles, resin, top: **$365**; *lower three:* **$225** *each.*

Weeks fruit and vegetable necklace, Bakelite charms on celluloid chain, ***$600****.*

*Evans bangles, resin, **$250** each.*

*Evans layered bangles, resin, **$195** each.*

*Evans hinged bangle with laminated rods of color, resin, **$250**.*

Shultz smoking-theme brooch, Bakelite and celluloid, **$850**.

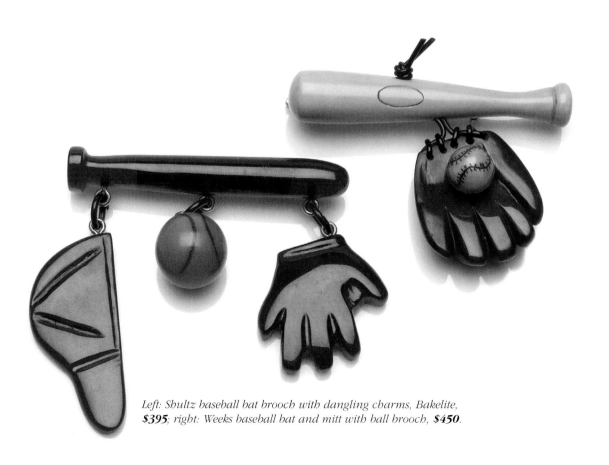

Left: Shultz baseball bat brooch with dangling charms, Bakelite,
$395*; right: Weeks baseball bat and mitt with ball brooch,* **$450**.

Evans octopus eye bangle, resin, **$195**.

Evans zigzag bangles, resin, **$195** *each.*

*Evans dot bangles, resin, top: **$235**; bottom left: **$195**; bottom middle: **$200**; bottom right: **$235**.*

*Evans checkerboard bangles, resin, top left: **$230**; top right: **$22**; bottom left: **$335**; bottom middle: **$335**; bottom right: **$325**.*

Shultz bangles, Bakelite, ***$1,400*** *each.*

Shultz polka-dot bangles, top: ***$650****; bottom left:* ***$650****; bottom right:* ***$675****.*

*Weeks fish and bobber necklace, Bakelite charms on celluloid chain, **$500**.*

*Clarke reverse-carved bangle with hand painting and rhinestones, Lucite, **$800**.*

*Clarke bangles, left: top and reverse-carved Lucite bangle, hand painted with rhinestones and glitter, **$750**; right: reverse-carved applejuice Bakelite with hand painting, **$1,500-$2,000**.*

*Clarke reverse-carved bangles, left: Lucite with hand painting, **$650**; middle: Lucite with hand painting and rhinestones, **$500**; right: applejuice Bakelite with hand painting, **$2,000**.*

*Shultz frog brooch with moving arm, Bakelite, **$600**.* *Shultz turtle brooch, Bakelite, **$350**.*

*Shultz lizard brooch, Bakelite, **$395**.*

*Shultz brooches, Bakelite, left: parrot with glass eye, **$550**; right: parrot with glass eye, **$900+**.*

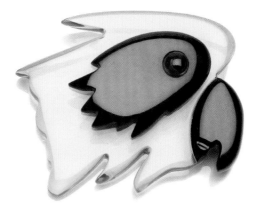

*Evans dog brooch, phenol resin, **$150**.*

*Shultz brooches, left: pig brooch, Bakelite, **$500**; right: cat brooch, Bakelite, **$350**.*

*Clarke butterscotch Bakelite bangle with amber beads, **$500**.*

*Shultz checkerboard bangle, applejuice Bakelite, **$900**.*

*Clarke top-carved bangle, marbled green Bakelite, **$800**.*

Weeks reverse-carved and painted applejuice Bakelite and orange Bakelite stretch bracelet, **$475***.*

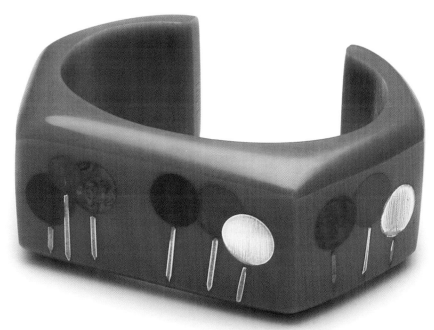

Weeks balloon design bangle, Bakelite, **$300***.*

Shultz dovetail bangle, Bakelite, ***$1,100***.

Left: Kronimus knife-edge bangles, Bakelite, ***$1,000*** *for set of three;*
right: Kronimus checkerboard bangle, Bakelite, ***$550***.

Shultz hand brooch with dot bangle, Bakelite, **$450**.

Weeks brooch, Bakelite with hand painting, **$400**.

Christine Pavone brooches, left: dog brooch, Galalith, **$95**; *right: cat brooch, Galalith,* **$95**.

Evans cherry brooch, resin, **$175**.

Shultz bird brooch, blue moon Bakelite, **$900+**.

*Contemporary Lea Stein hedgehog brooch, celluloid, **$50**.*

*Shultz dog and fire hydrant brooch, Bakelite, **$300**.*

*Adrian cactus brooch, Bakelite, **$600**.*

*Weeks brooch, carved Bakelite, **$500**.*

*Shultz bar brooch with hanging buttons and green balls, Bakelite, **$375**.*

*Shultz bear with balloons brooch, Bakelite, old inset dot eyes, **$375**.*

*Adrian merry-go-round brooch, Bakelite, **$500**.*

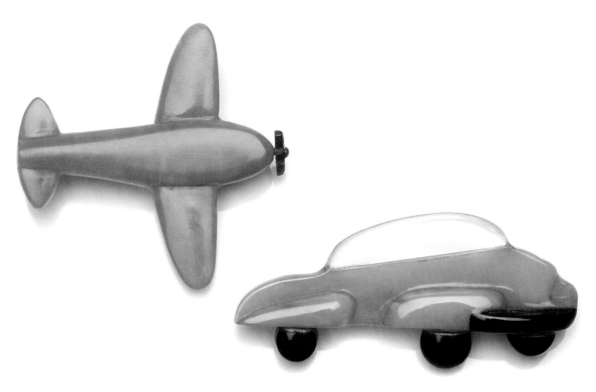

*Shultz brooches, left: airplane, Bakelite, **$375**; right: car, Bakelite, **$395**.*

*Top left: Adrian fish basket brooch, Bakelite, **$550**; top right: Shultz fish brooch with reverse-carved belly, Bakelite, **$350**; bottom: Shultz fish brooch, Bakelite, **$375**.*

Clarke Christmas tree brooch, Lucite with Bakelite, Lucite, and celluloid charms, **$250.**

Foltz Christmas tree brooch with Scotties and Bones, Bakelite, **$250**.

*Clarke Christmas tree brooches, acrylic with rhinestones and Bakelite and celluloid charms, **$250–$275** each.*

*Shultz Christmas tree brooches, Bakelite, from left: **$350**, **$375**, **$375**, **$350**.*

*Shultz bar brooch with hanging dice and dominoes, Bakelite, **$475**.*

*Shultz bow brooch with dangling charms, Bakelite, **$475**.*

*Shultz checkerboard hat brooch with Scotties, Bakelite, **$550**.*

*Shultz checkerboard heart brooch with Scotties, Bakelite, **$450**.*

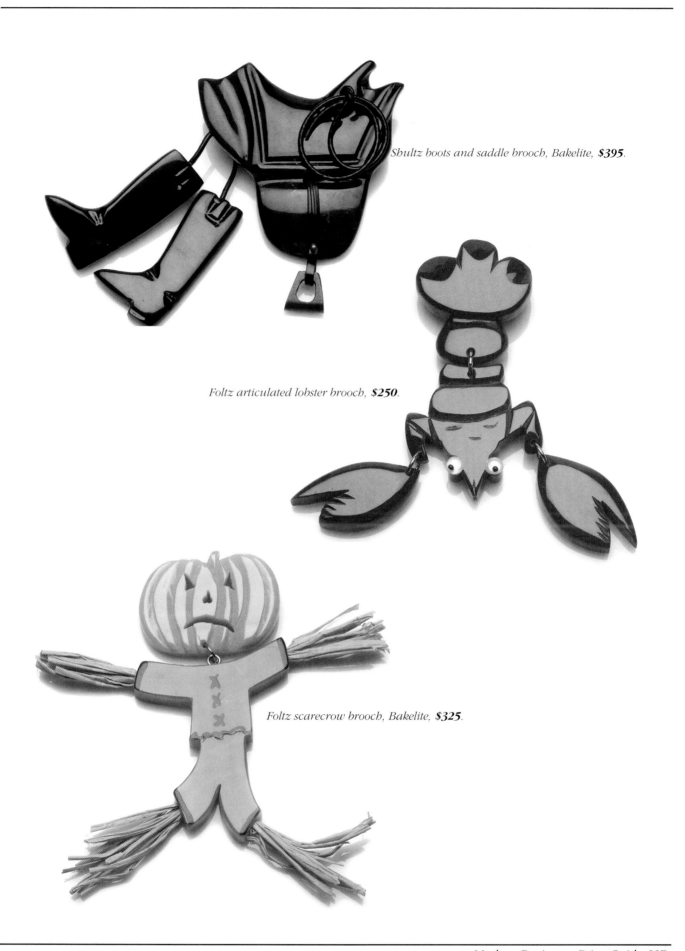

Shultz boots and saddle brooch, Bakelite, ***$395***.

Foltz articulated lobster brooch, ***$250***.

Foltz scarecrow brooch, Bakelite, ***$325***.

Foltz engraved Scottie bangle, butterscotch Bakelite, $135.

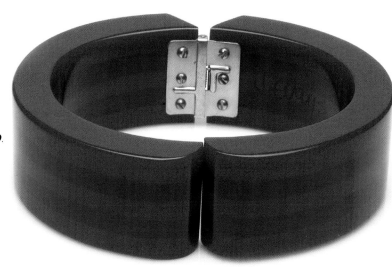

Evans hinged layered bangle, resin, $200.

Evans oval dot bangles, resin, $165 each.

*Shultz basket brooch with dangling fish, Bakelite, **$550**.*

*Weeks fish and bobber brooch, Bakelite, **$425**.*

*Foltz reverse-carved fishbowl brooch, applejuice Bakelite with hand painting, **$150**.*

*Left: laminated and reverse-carved fish bowl brooch, Bakelite, **$425**; right: Shultz reverse-carved bee jar brooch, Bakelite, **$425**.*

*Weeks matchstick brooch, Bakelite, **$425**.*

*Weeks Cigar brooch with dangling matches, Bakelite, **$450**.*

*Shultz Miami Beach brooch, Bakelite, **$500**.*

*Weeks brooch, Bakelite and celluloid chain, **$500**.*

*Shultz bird brooch, Bakelite, reverse-carved flowers with hand painting, **$375**.*

*Shultz brooches, left: peas and carrots, Bakelite, **$350**; right: double carrots, Bakelite, **$350**.*

*Weeks laminated Bakelite ring, **$225**.*

*Weeks lemon brooch, carved Bakelite, **$250**.*

Clarke reverse-carved bangle with hand painting, Lucite, **$650**.

Clarke reverse-carved bangle with hand painting, Lucite, **$650**.

*Clarke acrylic bangle with rhinestones and Majorca pearls, **$600**.*

Clarke top carved blue swirl Bakelite bangle with
*hand painting and rhinestones, **$900-$1,200**.*

*Foltz figural brooch, carved Bakelite with hand painting, **$135**.*

*Adrian beet brooch with dangling vegetables, Bakelite, **$900+**.*

*Clarke reverse-carved necklaces, Lucite with hand painting, celluloid chain, **$200** each.*

*Shultz figural brooches, Bakelite, **$350** each.*

*Shultz bar brooch with hanging rings, Bakelite and celluloid chain, **$425**.*

*Adrian dunce cap brooch with dangling charms,
Bakelite and celluloid, **$900+**.*

*Foltz Scottie dog in boat fishing brooch, carved Bakelite
with hand painting, **$135**.*

Foltz bone with hanging Scotties brooch, Bakelite, $195.

Foltz Scottie dog charm bracelet, Bakelite charms, $125.

Foltz cat brooch with mice charms, carved Bakelite with hand painting, $225.

Clarke reverse-carved bangle with hand painting, Lucite, **$650**.

Clarke reverse-carved bangle with hand painting, Lucite, **$650**.

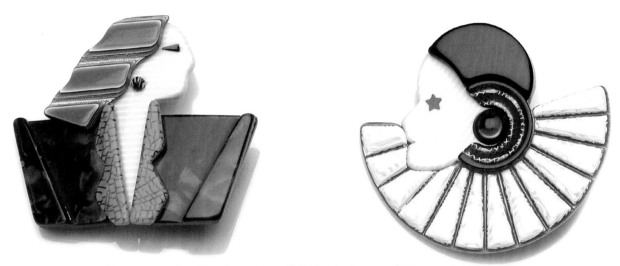

*Contemporary Lea Stein brooches, celluloid, left: Carmen, **$70**; right: Colerette, **$60**.*

*Contemporary Lea Stein women brooches, celluloid, **$100** each.*

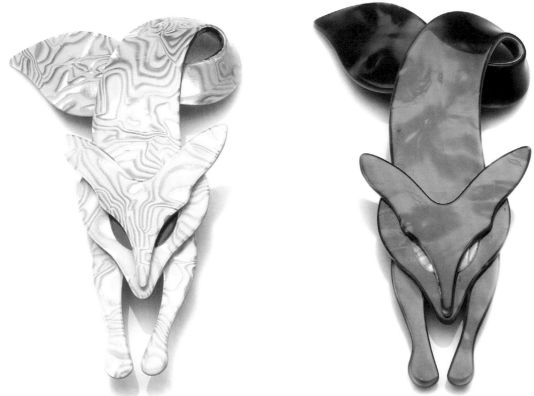

Contemporary Lea Stein fox brooches, celluloid, from left: **$55**, **$60**.

Contemporary Lea Stein earring and brooch set, celluloid, left: Attila, **$90**; *right: Gomina,* **$86**.